THE CUP THAT I DRINK

Also by Gerald O'Mahony

ABBA! FATHER!
A personal catechism of the Catholic faith

Cover illustration: The Last Supper (detail) by
Sr Angelica Ballan PD. © PDDM Apostolato
Liturgico, Rome. By courtesy of the Sisters Disciples
of the Divine Master.

Gerald O'Mahony S.J.

THE CUP
THAT I DRINK

Thoughts and prayers
about the chalice

St Paul Publications

St Paul Publications
Middlegreen, Slough SL3 6BT, England

Copyright © 1985 Trustees for Roman Catholic Purposes Registered
First published June 1985
Printed by the Society of St Paul, Slough
ISBN 085439 240 8

St Paul Publications is an activity of the priests and brothers
of the Society of St Paul who promote the Christian message through
the mass media

To my cousin
Marie O'Mahony
who helped me put pen to paper
in the dark days

*'God is the goodness
that may not be angry,
for he is
nothing but goodness.'*

Julian of Norwich

Contents

Introduction

Very few devotional books have ever been written for Roman
Catholics who receive the chalice at the Eucharist. For many centuries, until the publication of the new Roman Missal in 1970,
communion under both kinds was reserved to the priests. As a
result, most of the devotional works written to help the laity enter
into the mystery of the Eucharist took it for granted that they would
be receiving under the form of bread alone. The images and ex-
amples and texts used by the authors were biased heavily in favour
of 'food' rather than 'drink'. The main feast celebrating the
Eucharist was called *Corpus Christi*, The Body of Christ. Only
since 1970 has it been called 'The Body and Blood of Christ'.

A book like the present one could equally be accused of having
a bias in favour of the chalice, but my purpose is really only to try
and redress the balance a little. The imagery and meanings of the
cup are so beautiful, we all need to be more conscious of them.
Many Roman Catholics, apart perhaps from the first day they
received the chalice, may have had no homilies or sermons to guide
their minds and hearts into this new aspect of the mystery. Here,
then, hopefully, they will find a guide. The short chapters are
divided into a section of instruction or inspiration, followed by a
prayer or prayers. Priests and teachers also may find here material
to help them give a place to the riches of the chalice in their
homilies, sermons and lessons. This is for anyone who receives the
chalice, and for anyone who desires to receive the chalice.

Perhaps a further word is called for, as a reference point for
much of what follows: There may seem to be a confusion in the
writing, once the materials of the Eucharist, the bread, water and
wine, are traced back to their original symbolism, as to whether we
are trying to divide the indivisible Christ. Jesus living in Galilee or
Judaea was undivided; only in his death was his blood (and the
water) separated from his body (Jn 19:34). In the resurrection
Jesus is one and undivided, one divine person whose body is a

'Spiritual' body, as we may infer from St Paul (1 Cor 15:44): In the Eucharist we receive the risen Christ, 'whole and entire' whether in the form of bread or in the form of wine, though the words of consecration, 'separating' the blood from the body in the manner of Our Lord's words at the Last Supper, make present the one sacrifice of Christ, 'in an unbloody manner'.

Each human person has from the beginning of history been one and undivided in himself. Philosophers in different ages and cultures have seemed (only seemed) to divide that unity into sections, differently according to different ways of thinking. The pattern followed in this book and taken from the early Fathers of the Church is that of speaking of man as *body, human spirit, divine spirit*, corresponding to the three symbols *bread, water, wine*. By *divine spirit* in ordinary men and women I mean the same as supernatural grace. Even before the coming of Jesus, the Holy Spirit was already at work by grace in each person, and one might say that each person had (what Karl Rahner calls a *potentia obedientialis*) a capacity, but not a right, to become a child of God. My own way of speaking of this capacity, in symbols, would be to say that 'the grape was already here on earth, long before the coming of wine in the fullness of time'. Wine came 'from above', an unsuspected blessing, a total surprise; water comes from below, from wells within the earth (Gen 2:6), as does the body itself, from the dust of the earth (Gen 2:7).

In the early Fathers, both bread and the human body are spoken of as being 'made by human hands' and as coming 'from the earth' or 'from below'. If I will seem to make much of the liturgical use of water in the Eucharist, considering how little water we add to the wine nowadays, I make no apology. According to the great liturgical scholar Fr Joseph Jungmann, the mixing of water with wine was a practice observed in Palestine in Christ's time;[1] the early Church writers frequently speak in terms of 'the mingled cup', meaning wine with much more than a drop of water;[2] the Eastern Church to this day uses far more water in the chalice than we in the West do; and most importantly, the symbolism I attach in these pages to the water in the Eucharist (as *human spirit*) has a long and honourable

[1] *The Mass of the Roman Rite*, London 1959; p. 333.
[2] E.g. Irenaeus, *Against the Heresies*, V 2:3.

ancestry, as long as christianity itself. We may now use only a drop of water, but the Catholic Church has never allowed this use of water to be abandoned.

To speak of Jesus himself as *bread, water* and *wine* is a way of speaking of the one divine person Jesus, as having a fully human nature (with therefore a body and human spirit) and his divine nature. If at one time or another I will seem to stress one aspect or another of the Jesus we know from the gospels and from our personal experience, I only intend to follow St Ignatius of Loyola in his *Spiritual Exercises*, where for example in the Contemplations on the Passion he alerts the exercitant to 'consider how the divinity hides itself' (§196), but in the Contemplations on the Resurrection his advice is 'to consider the divinity, which seemed to hide itself during the passion, now appearing and manifesting itself so miraculously in its true and most sacred effects' (§223).

Lastly, a word about redemption. Jesus died 'for the many', that is, for everyone. Therefore, he died for me as much as for anyone else. Conversely, I believe, if he did not die for me, he died for no one. If I seem to imply that Jesus' death so long ago is somehow 'my fault' (or 'our fault'), I only wish to use the words as a child might in looking back after being saved by a strong swimmer who himself drowned in the rescue.

1

The cup that I drink

When did Jesus speak about 'the cup that I drink'? According to the gospels of Matthew and Mark, he spoke thus about the cup or chalice while on his way to Jerusalem and to death. Peter had tried to stop Jesus from heading so resolutely into danger, and had been rebuked for interfering. Jesus was now walking ahead of his followers, who were troubled and hanging back. Then the apostles James and John approached Jesus and asked him to grant them a favour: could they sit, one at his right hand and the other at his left hand, in the kingdom? Jesus replied by asking them, 'Are you able to drink the cup that I drink?' They said, 'We are able'. Jesus agreed: they would indeed drink his cup, but it was not in his power to give them places on either side of him at his victory celebrations. The Father would decide who sat in which place.

'The cup that I drink ... ' Jesus' twelve apostles were unable, at that time, to foresee what kind of cup Jesus was thinking of. He himself must have had a pretty clear idea. The cup was his passion; the cup was all he would have to undergo, to fulfil his Father's will for the salvation of mankind. Not one of the twelve was able to accompany Jesus when he actually drank his cup of suffering. Instead, they all ran away. Later, they were given strength, and then James was the first of all the twelve to be martyred. John underwent sufferings of his own for the sake of his beloved Master, but in the end lived through to old age and a natural death.

Every Christian can take this request of James and John and apply it to himself or herself. The cup that Jesus drinks is offered to all Christians who wish to follow him as disciples. Jesus, so to speak, takes the cup and drinks from it, then offers it to his disciple. In taking the cup and drinking from it, we do not condemn ourselves to a martyr's death. Of the two disciples with whom Jesus first spoke about sharing his cup, one became a martyr but the

1

other did not. The chalice will mean a different destiny for each one who drinks of it. Even Jesus cannot guarantee what place in the kingdom of heaven my own destiny will give me. St Paul reminds us that 'star differs from star in glory' (1 Cor 15:41); heaven would be unbalanced if all the stars wanted to be in the one place, all shining with exactly the same colour and intensity. Most of the sky would be left dark. How much better the wisdom of God, who allots to each star its place in the heavens.

One of the psalms contains a prayer of praise to the God whom we know as our Father: 'O Lord, it is you who are my portion and cup; it is you yourself who are my prize. The lot marked out for me is my delight: welcome indeed the heritage that falls to me!' (Ps 15[16]: 5f). How very differently that same psalm sounds to us when we are well and when we are ill, when we are freewheeling downhill and when we are struggling uphill. When we are in distress, it seems to us that Jesus drank his share a long, long time ago, and has left us to drink our share, the bitter dregs, on our own. When we are at peace and being consoled by God, then indeed the lot marked out for us feels delightful, our heritage is most welcome. As the chalice was passed round the apostles at the Last Supper they shared with Jesus before his death, how different were to be the destinies of each apostle. At our own celebrations of the Eucharist, as one after another of the congregation accepts the chalice and drinks from it, how different are the lives and destinies of each. Each of us has secrets known only to God. We, like the twelve apostles, have to be reminded not to be ambitious to sit in someone else's place, since the place chosen for each one by our Father will suit that one, and that one alone, perfectly.

Prayer of one receiving the chalice

My Lord Jesus, when your apostles James and John boasted so confidently to you, 'Yes, we can drink the same chalice you drink', they did not know what they were saying. But I have seen your passion and death, and I know what your cup held for you. Can I find the strength to take your cup? Only if I may share it with you, then I will be strong enough to take it; only if I receive it from your hands, will it ever bring me joy. All too often, the joys go by in my life and I forget that they, too, are part of my chalice and

2

destiny. All too often, when I am in trouble or distress, the trouble has come about as a result of my own stupidity or carelessness, and then I feel I have no right to think of my sorrows as being joined together with your sorrows. Remind me, my Master, that you are bound to me as my brother, and whatever I do, be it wise or stupid, be it good or bad, is of vital interest to you because you are my brother. Likewise, if you are the shepherd and I am the sheep, then it makes no difference to you if it was through stupidity that I got lost: sheep are well known for being stupid, so the shepherd expects as much.

When all goes well, and I am conscious of your nearness, then your chalice is my delight. Then I seem to be sharing your own Last Supper: the cup was passed round the apostles and has been handed round ever since, until it comes to me. Then I seem to be close to you, at your right hand or at your left. I am being invited to join in the greatest adventure of all time, to share with you in the redemption of all humankind, and to have my own personal share in your work.

But whether I do well or badly, you can still make use of my offering. The cup is yours, the salvation is from you. My own journey can take strange, unexpected turns. But so long as I love you and come back to you, whatever happens can bring about good through the workings of your Father's providence.

Heavenly Father, 'it is you who are my portion and cup, it is you yourself who are my prize'. When Jesus took his cup, he was accepting your will for him. When I in my turn take the cup, then with Jesus I am accepting your will for me. 'The lot marked out for me is my delight: welcome indeed the heritage that falls to me!' Your will for me, Father, is my destiny, my lot, my heritage. Make me always welcome the things that happen to me, and let me not pick and choose among your gifts to me. Even the most unhappy days can teach me something about your love: in those days I learn to see the pattern of your work, for if I wait, then in time you always return, as surely as spring follows winter.

'You are my portion and cup, you yourself are my prize.' As the father in Jesus' parable said to his elder son, so you say to me, 'You are always with me, and all that is mine is yours'. How futile my worries must appear to you at times!

3

2
Remove this cup

Even Jesus did not always find the lot marked out for him to be delightful. The night before he suffered, he was in an agony of dread as he prayed in the garden of Gethsemane. His prayer went like this, according to St Mark: 'Abba, Father, all things are possible to you, remove this cup from me; yet not what I want, but what you want' (Mk 14:36). Peter, James and John had been invited to stay close and to watch with him; so it comes about that we know the words Jesus used in this prayer, whereas nearly all his other private prayers to his Father are his own secret. From this prayer, we can understand something of what St Paul is referring to when he writes about our receiving 'the spirit of adoption, by which we cry out "Abba, Father!"' (Rom 8:15) The three apostles were able at Gethsemane to hear the familiar way in which Jesus addressed his Father, and to pass on to others the invitation from Jesus that we share his Father as our very own, even in suffering.

'All things are possible to you, remove this cup from me.' When we think of any father or mother in our experience, we know they would most certainly remove the painful or harmful obstacles from the path of their children, if they could. If a young child has to go to hospital, and in hospital pleads with his parents to take him home with them, they certainly would take him home, if they could. But he must have his operation or he will die; and so they leave him in hospital until the operation is safely over. Similarly, we can be sure God would remove pain and other evils from our path if he could. If the pain remains, it must be because for some good reason God cannot remove it. Why could Jesus' Father not remove the chalice from him? The Father did not want Jesus to die, but he did want Jesus to witness the sort of God he is. The only way of escape for Jesus, there in the garden at the eleventh hour, would have been to flee for his life, back to Galilee and obscurity. Jesus would have borne witness to a God who runs away rather than stand by his flock, his little ones. 'My Father, if it be possible, let this cup pass from me' (Mt 26:39), was the prayer of Jesus according to St Matthew, and the cup did not pass. We can only conclude that it was not possible for it to pass from him there and then. He would have to drink it first, and then the power of God would be shown.

'Yet not what I want, but what you want.' His Father wanted, not the death of Jesus but his truth and loyalty. Being true to his Father led Jesus straight to his death, which was the last thing either he or his Father wanted. Jesus was able to stretch his heart over the painful death to the thing both he and his Father did want: that the people of the world should come to know how much God loves them, even in the midst of their sins. How many of us can lift our hearts over the aspects of our lives that we hate, to where our Father and we are in agreement? The prayer of Jesus in the garden is a constant source of comfort to those who are in distress. It reminds us first of all of the loving kindness of God who wants to be called our Father, and therefore it reminds us he wishes us no harm. If something pains us, we are invited to pray, like Jesus, that if possible this chalice may pass from us, and to abandon the matter into our Father's hands. If even then the chalice is not taken away, perhaps as in the case of Jesus there may be some greater, far greater, good at stake which we cannot yet see. So then in blindness we have the company of Jesus as we drink the cup.

Prayer of one in distress

Abba! Father! Jesus called you by that name, the same name that Hebrew-speaking children to this day call their own fathers: Abba! May I then call you by the same name I and my brothers and sisters called our father at home? My Father, since you are my Father, I can only believe that you mean me well. If pain and distress and trouble come my way, I know that they are either none of your doing, or else they are unavoidable stepping-stones to something far outweighing them in importance. Even if they are none of your doing, but only the result of someone else's thoughtlessness or my own folly, I believe you can make them stepping-stones to something great.

But the anguish is hard to bear, my Father. In my sorrow I feel as though nobody else ever had a sorrow quite like mine. Looking back, I can see how nearly this tragedy never happened at all — why then did it have to happen? Too late now to go back and take the steps that would have avoided it. Please, take my sorrow away from me. All power is yours, and I believe you will take away my distress and heal my heart if this is at all possible. Let my sorrow not remain with me for want of my asking you to take it away! Please, take my sorrow away from me. But if there is no escape from this cup, and I must drink it, give me the comfort of knowing I do your will. Perhaps I ought never to have arrived where I am: do you from now on please call me, so that I may share this cup with your Son. Let the cup remind me always that every sorrow in this life has an end, either now or in the world to come. And if I drink this cup with your Son, then I and those whom I have lost will find one another again in his glory.

Jesus, my brother, I feel for your deep anguish the night before your passion. What a great comfort to me now, your anguish. Who ever faced so terrible a death as yours with such powers of imagination as you had, to guess what it would be like? I can think of all the events in my own life that I have dreaded beforehand, often finding in the event that they were bearable after all. But in my present sorrow I find comfort and companionship in your fear and sweat in the Garden. The divine Son of God actually knows what I feel like, and from an experience far more bitter than mine! For you, the question was how to face death. For us, the question usually is how to face life again, after a bereavement, an accident, an illness, a disgrace of some sort. But the day comes when we too must face death. Then your voice calling to us is our comfort: 'I was dead, but now I am alive!' (cf. Rev 1 : 18). You even seem in some sense to return, and though you can suffer no more, yet in me you are suffering still. My sufferings are yours. You carry me on eagles' wings, because you alone of all the voices in this world can make any sense of my suffering.

Jesus my friend, if there is an honourable way round this suffering, or a cure that I have overlooked, please enlighten me,

6

give me wisdom and strength. But if I must drink the chalice and find it bitter, then please, my brother, let me drink it with you and in you.

3

A share in the chalice

Because of our Baptism and Confirmation, every Christian has a place at God's table, and a share in the chalice. Our Baptism celebrates God's gift to us of himself as our Father; it gives us a place at his table which can never be taken away from us, and the bread of the children; it calls for our faith and trust, since God is saying, 'Believe in my love for you'; God's voice from heaven says (as to Jesus at his Baptism), 'You are my beloved child. My favour rests on you'. Baptism celebrates that we are God's sheep or lambs, that his light shines on us, that we are built on his rock, that we are fish in his net, and a field sown with seed, that we are guided along the way, and waited upon by God.

Confirmation, on the other hand, celebrates God's call, the fact that he never ceases to call us; it gives us a share in the chalice — our own share, unlike anyone else's; it calls for our love in response to God's goodness, since God is saying, 'Love others as I have loved you'; God's voice from heaven says (as to Jesus at his transfiguration), 'This is my beloved child. Listen to him' or 'Listen to her'. Confirmation celebrates God's calling me to be now a shepherd, a light for others, a foundation stone, a fisher of men, a fruitful tree or field, a good guide, a servant or slave to others.

Many Catholics today would argue that Baptism and Confirmation are best seen as one sacrament. If ever the sacrament of Confirmation is taken over by a revised rite of Baptism, then inevitably the sacrament of Baptism will be a sacrament with two aspects, and the two aspects will be those here described as belonging to Baptism and Confirmation. God's gift to us must come first: we are only called and drawn to serve him because his gift came first. Faith is the beginning, the end is love. My candle must be lit by God before I can enlighten others. I must learn what it is to be a lamb and a sheep before I can make a good shepherd. I must be built on rock before I can dare to support others. We have always described Baptism as being 'necessary for salvation' and Confirmation as being a voluntary sacrament. Our salvation depends on our accepting the gift of God's love and mercy; our attempts to thank him by imitating his ways will always be so poor that our salvation could never rest on them.

We may say, then, that our Baptism gives us a sure place of our own at God's table, and for our food the bread of the children (cf. Mk 7:27); our Confirmation gives us a share in the chalice, meaning a share in the responsibility as well. What responsibility? The responsibility to be like our Father. Each of us is a different image of the same Father, so each one of us will find a different destiny in the cup.

Jesus asked James and John, 'Are you able to drink the cup that I drink, or to be baptized with the baptism with which I am baptized?' (Mk 10:38). On that occasion Jesus seemed to include the responsibility and the sacrifice under the word 'baptism'. When we read that verse of the gospel, we have to include in Jesus' meaning not only what we understand by Baptism, but also what we understand by Confirmation. A full initiation for a Christian includes all those elements. The fullness of Baptism is found in our loving response to God's unfailing kindness.

Prayer of a Christian

Loving Father, may I thank you for calling me out of nothingness to be your child? I thank you for placing me in your own family, where forgiveness rules and no sinner is condemned. For you have given me your own Son for my brother, and sent him to look for me and search me out. And at what a cost he found me, the cost of his own life's blood! You have given me a place at your table, with my own name on it. Even if I desert you and go away, that place will always be kept empty against the day of my return. You will never allow my place to be removed or given to anyone else. For my food, you give me the bread of life, the body of your own Son present in mystery, the bread of the children. I am not one of your chosen people of old, nor am I a worthy member of the new Israel, but you give me the bread reserved for your own children. You give me your Spirit: all the love that proceeds from you to your own Son, you have given to me, so that now the Spirit comes from you to me, calling me everlastingly your own son (your own daughter). This is the water of which I can never drink enough, nor ever drink too much: your Spirit given to me. For these and all your gifts I thank you, my Father.

THE CHRISTIAN SPEAKS TO JESUS: Jesus, my Teacher, tell me 'How can I repay the Lord for his goodness to me?' (Ps 115[116]: 12).

JESUS REPLIES: 'Take the cup of salvation, call on God's name', as the psalm tells you. Take the cup which I drink, and do not be afraid. Ask my Father, and he will see to it that you are not tempted beyond your strength. He will temper the wind to the shorn lamb, until you grow strong in his service. See, he is calling you to learn to be a shepherd, and to look after his sheep, his yearlings and his lambs. You, with your sisters and brothers, will become the light of the world, as I was the light of the world in the days of my flesh. I will continue to shine through you my disciples. He is calling you to be a rock of support to those who come to you: his love for you can weather any storm, and so now your love for the weak and helpless can afford to be everlasting. He had guided you through me: now you will guide others. He and I have been your servant: now you will serve others.

The Spirit was mine, and I gave him to you. My love, my service and loyalty to my Father's will now become yours. When you, in me, love and serve my Father, then the Spirit proceeds from you to the Father. Do not be afraid. Remember you are for all eternity my lamb, and as such you can always be saved, even if through weakness you fail to become a good shepherd.

THE CHRISTIAN REPLIES: Father, Son and Spirit, who am I that you make me the temple where you dwell? I know now, my Father, how I can repay you for your goodness to me. 'I will raise the cup of salvation', and try to serve you worthily in return for your great goodness, by bringing your constant love to others.

10

4

Bread, water and wine

When a priest at the Eucharist is mixing a drop of water into the chalice of wine, he says quietly to himself this prayer: 'By the mystery of this water and wine, may we come to share in the divinity of Christ, who humbled himself to share in our humanity'. Why is that prayer appropriate for that moment? The background to the prayer is the traditional way Christians have, of comparing bread to the human body, water to the human spirit or life, and wine to the divine life. There are other ways of mentally dividing up the reality which is a human being, but this one of referring to 'your whole being, spirit, soul and body' (1 Thess 5 : 23) is a common one in the early Church.

Men and women by themselves and unredeemed could be represented by the bread 'made with hands' and by the water: a human body with a purely human life. The divine Son of God as he was before the incarnation could be represented by wine. We were 'bread and water'; he was divine 'wine'. When the Son takes our human nature to himself, his wine is mingled with our water and bread, so that eventually he, and we, could become bread, water and wine. He and we become a new creation, fully human but alive with a divine life.

Water in Christian symbolism has many meanings: the Spirit, the waters of baptism, waters of destruction, waters of life. In the prayer at the mixing of water and wine at Mass, the water has the same meaning as the water which was turned into wine at Cana in Galilee. There, in the first of the signs that Jesus performed, he turned jars of water into jars of wine. Jesus was proclaiming that he had come to turn human life into divine life, to raise our lives to a completely new level. 'Spirit, soul and body, your whole being', said St Paul. The wine in the chalice stands for the 'spirit' in us, our divine life as children of God, the supernatural life, our rela-

11

tionships with the Trinity. The water stands for our own unaided life and mind — something we have never actually seen, since grace has always been working in us even before we were conscious of it.

The process by which we are changed into the image of Christ is as old as creation in its origins. His own birth at Bethlehem is a key-point in the story. His death and resurrection is the climax of the story. But playing its own part, day by day and week by week, is the Eucharist. We believe that Jesus Christ is present equally in the bread of life and in the chalice, but the ancient symbolism has not lost its power, and those who take the chalice are visibly reminded that the divine life of our Redeemer is slowly and lovingly being transferred to us.

'Blessed are you, Lord God of all creation. Through your goodness we have this wine to offer. . . It will become our spiritual drink.' So prays the priest quietly at the offertory of the Mass. This is the drink that will be, in symbol and in truth, the gift of the spirit, the gift of Christ's divine life to us. This is the same spiritual drink that St Paul saw foretold in the 'spiritual drink' the chosen people drank from the rock, 'and the rock was Christ' (1 Cor 10:4). The third Eucharistic Prayer contains the following passage: 'Grant that we, who are nourished by his body and blood, may be filled with his Holy Spirit, and become one body, one spirit in Christ'. Through the body of Christ, we become one body; through his blood we become one spirit.

Prayer of wonder to the Lord Jesus

Jesus, my Saviour, how cramped and confined your spirit must have felt, sharing our human condition! How slow we must always be, to understand what you are telling us and what you are doing for us. And yet how endlessly patient a teacher you are.

Who but you would have agreed to such an exchange? You alone were God's own Son, but you never asked for any special treatment in our world. You alone were pure wine, yet you took on our bread-and-water lives without a word of complaint. You were the Servant, servant of God your Father because he wanted us all to share your divine sonship, and that is why he sent you. You were the servant of us all, because you put aside your own convenience and your own ambitions and even your own life in an effort to make us see how much your Father loves us. Man thought he had silenced you when you were dead on the cross, but our cruellest effort is no match for your goodness: your Father raised you and sent you back to us from beyond the grave, to show that not even then would he cease to love us and invite us.

You must have felt cramped in our company, though you never complained. Yet we never cease to complain as you raise us in our turn to share in your divine life. The bread-and-water which is our condition finds itself stretched as it is mingled with the wine of your divine life. We start out in great delight at such an invitation, to be God's son or God's daughter. But then we get side-tracked, or tempted by lesser delights along the way, because your invitation means a journey to a distant land. Persecutions or troubles or sickness come our way, and we lose heart, thinking that surely wine was never meant to taste like this. But how could we poor mortals know what immortal life tastes like? We have never before tasted such wine: it should be enough for us that you invite us to the cup. You suffered so much in sharing our life; can we expect to share yours with no pain? We had no power to support you in drinking your cup, but you have power to keep us in your hand as we drink our cup.

Help me to look again at the trials and sorrows of my life, and to see in them the wine that you are offering me. Help me to be like the blind Bartimaeus whom you cured of his blindness, so that he followed you on the way. Let me hear, as he heard in his blindness, the voice of those who say, 'Take heart; get up; he is calling you' (Mk 10:49). These are not death-traps into which you are calling me. These sorrows are the birth pangs of your new life in me. You were cramped and confined in our life: we will be stretched and our hearts expanded as we make room for your life. Why cannot I, why cannot all your Father's children, seem to be drunk with the gift of your Spirit, as were the apostles and disciples at the first Pentecost: 'They are filled with new wine' (Acts 2:13)?

5

Pierced by a lance

St John in his gospel tells the story of how the saying of the prophet Zechariah was fulfilled: 'They will look on the one whom they have pierced; they will mourn for him as for an only son, and weep for him as people weep for a first-born child' (Zech 12:10). When Jesus was dying, he said, 'It is accomplished'; then he bowed his head and 'gave up his spirit'. Soon afterwards, the soldiers came to speed up the death of those who were crucified. They broke the legs of the two criminals on either side of Jesus, but when they came to Jesus and saw he was already dead, one of the soldiers pierced his side with a lance, and immediately there came out blood and water. Jesus gave up his spirit, and in death he gave up water and blood. His life, both human and divine, was poured out for us.

We re-enact the everlasting truth of these moments on Golgotha as we celebrate the Eucharist. We do as Jesus told his apostles to do: we take the bread and say in the name of Jesus, 'This is my body'. We take the chalice with the mixed water and wine, and say, 'This is my blood'. Jesus is living now beyond the reach of death, but according to the words he left us, his body is *here*, his blood and the water is *there*, thus signifying his death. The words of the sacrament make present to our minds and hearts the time when his body was on the cross, but his blood was all spilt for us. There is something so final about the statement of John, 'there came out blood and water', as if there was no longer a drop of blood for him to give, but still he would go on giving.

How is it each of us can say, 'Jesus died for me; he shed his blood for me; he was pierced for me'? This is a question well worth answering for ourselves, well worth pondering often. Something rebellious in us keeps nagging, 'I never asked him to die for me. His death makes no difference to me'. Jesus died because he would not let anyone be shut out from God's fatherhood or God's mercy. Jesus, Son of God, treated all men, women and children as his divine brothers and sisters. He was condemned and handed over to Pilate for blasphemy (Mk 14:64); but it was his popularity which brought him to the notice of the authorities in the first place, and that popularity came about because he was so wide and effective in his sympathies (e.g., Mk 3:6ff; 7:1).

The gospel stories invite the reader to say, 'If I am a leper, Jesus does not shut me out; if I am blind, he will show me the way; if I am shut out by society for being a foreigner, or a criminal, I am not shut out of his kingdom; if I am exploited because I am a woman, or a child, or a servant, Jesus will treat me as an equal, and he will welcome me into his kingdom as an equal. If I am conscious of being a sinner, he will forgive me and restore me to my place at my Father's table'. With the Good News firmly planted in my heart, I can hold up my head in any company, humbly but with confidence. The blessings of his gospel are with me every day, but they cost Jesus his life-blood. He was persecuted because he refused to make any exceptions, but instead welcomed into his kingdom anyone at all who would accept God's forgiveness and refrain from judging others. If his enemies had known of me and had wanted to shut me out, he would have died rather than let them do so. The gospel message is alive today, helping me today, because Jesus staked his life on the truth of it, and his Father showed Jesus was right by raising him from the dead and showing him to the chosen witnesses.

One of the witnesses of his death was his own mother Mary. 'They will look on the one whom they have pierced; they will mourn for him as for an only son, and weep for him as people weep for a first-born child.' Perhaps this moment above all was for Mary the fulfilment of the strange saying of Simeon: 'And a sword will pierce your own soul too' (Lk 2:35).

Prayer for 'a heart of flesh'

Mary, mother of Jesus, and by his gift my mother too, I ask you to obtain for me from your Son and my Lord, the gift of 'a heart of flesh' that was promised in the scriptures (Ezek 36:26). Ask him to take away my heart of stone and to give me a heart of flesh. I need the courage to look without wavering at his death on the cross, and the last callous act of his killers, in piercing his side with a lance. He suffered this for me: I know if I had been the only one shut out by men from God's mercy, he would still have done all this for me, the least of his little ones. I need a heart of flesh, not a heart of stone, to stand and see how you mourned for your only son, how you wept for your first-born child. For a Jewish mother, for any mother, to watch her only son being executed for something he was never guilty of, what a grief that must have been. In the middle of it all, he gave his murderers to you as sons, he gave me to you as a son, and your heart was wide enough to accept us for his sake. Ask him, please (come with me now) to give me a heart as wide as yours in its affections.

Jesus, merciful Redeemer, see me standing with your mother, and asking you to obtain for me from your Father and mine the gift he promised. I want him to take out of my flesh the heart of stone and to give me a heart of flesh. May I never again be bored or unconcerned because you died for me. May I be aware of how completely you love me and trust me, though I have never given you much reason to trust me — far from it. You loved me to the last drop of your blood. As I receive the chalice, may I be forever grateful, and anxious to love you in return. May I love you by imitating you, by leaving no one outside my love. I want to welcome, as you did, foreigners and people of other races, friends and enemies, the sick and the handicapped, the sinners and the criminals, the exploited and the outcasts. I want to work with others in the communities to which I belong, to bring about a society in this world from which no single person is shut out. How very far my present life is from such an ideal. See, then, how much I need this gift. Your disciple John tells us in his *Revelation* that you cannot stand those who are lukewarm (cf. Rev 3:15f). Come then with me to our Father, and ask with me for a warm heart, a heart after your own heart.

Father of love, in the name of Jesus your Son I ask for the gift of a heart of flesh. Put your Spirit within me, to make my heart full of sympathy and my hands ready to support. This life of ours is so short, at the close of it we will surely say, 'Life is over already, and how little I have done to thank my Father!' Give me a heart full of gratitude, one that sees what others have done and are doing for me. Let me never forget your Son, how his side was pierced with a lance for me. May I never cease to feel for his mother Mary in her sorrow. Let me never be so busy that I forget what my parents and so many other loving people did for me as a baby and as a child and until I left home. May I never take for granted the work other people do for me. Help me wherever possible to show my gratitude in deeds rather than in words. Make my sympathies ever wider, to take in my town, my country, the whole world of so many peoples. And above all, give me a tender heart towards yourself, my Father.

6

Fruit of the tree of life

According to St Luke writing in the *Acts of the Apostles*, the apostle Peter referred to the cross of Jesus as 'the tree'. Preaching to the centurion Cornelius and his family, Peter says about Jesus, 'They put him to death by hanging him on a tree' (Acts 10:39). St Paul has a similar way of speaking, when he says in the synagogue of Antioch in Pisidia, 'And when they had fulfilled all that was written of him, they took him down from the tree, and laid him in a tomb' (Acts 13:29). Now the two apostles may have been thinking of the passage in the scriptures that says, 'Cursed be the one who is hanged on a tree' (Deut 21:23), since St Paul certainly makes the connection in one of his letters, saying that Jesus was so cursed to free mankind from the curse of the law (Gal 3:13). It may simply have been the local custom in Jerusalem to refer to any cross used by the Romans for crucifixion as a 'tree'. Or the apostles may already have been thinking of the cross as the tree of life and of Jesus as the fruit of the tree of life, a comparison often made by Christian writers from very early times.

The comparison goes like this: in the story of the fall of man, in the book of *Genesis*, Adam and Eve eat the forbidden fruit of the tree of the knowledge of good and evil. The serpent had tempted Eve saying, 'You will not die . . . you will be like gods, knowing good and evil'. So they ate the fruit, and were driven out of the garden of Eden lest they should stretch out their hands and eat the fruit of the tree of life as well, and live for ever. The way to the tree of life was from then on barred to them by the flaming sword of the cherubim (Gen 3:24). But in the book of *Revelation*, at the far end of the bible, Jesus is described as saying, 'To him who conquers I will grant to eat of the tree of life, which is in the paradise of God'. The tree of life is found on the banks of the river of the water of life (sparkling like crystal) which flows through the new Jerusalem, and there are no orders about not eating from it.

All the trees praised by Jesus in his parables have this in common, that their fruit is somehow useful to man. The vine produces the grape, which is crushed to make 'the blood of the grape', wine for man to drink. (Three times in the Old Testament wine is described as 'the blood' of the grape.) The olive tree produces olives, which are crushed to make oil for the use of man. The fig produces fruit to be enjoyed. So too with the smaller plants: corn and the like produce seeds which are useful for human beings.

In the Eucharist we have preserved for us, till the end of time, the moment when the barren tree of the cross was made fruitful, when the fruit of the vine was on the tree, the Lord Jesus himself. He was crushed, and the blood 'of the grape' flowed from him, for ever useful to humankind. Fittingly, then, we may compare the cross, and the Eucharist, to the tree of life, whose fruit is no longer forbidden, and in whose wine is life for ever.

In the fruit of this tree we also find the fulfilment of that other dream which tempted Eve and Adam: 'You will be like gods'. Those who eat and drink the fruit of this tree do so because they are already children of God, each with their own place at his family table. In it we have a foretaste of paradise, where all that was lost in the beginning will be found again, and will exceed all our dreams.

A prayer of faith

JESUS THE TEACHER SPEAKS: This will be for many a rather far-fetched comparison, to say that I upon the cross shedding my life-blood from my body am like the tree of life with its fruit yielding new wine. Tell me what you think when you hear this comparison. What does it say to you, underneath the pictures and the strange language?

THE DISCIPLE REPLIES: You yourself, my Master, used language no less strange when you spoke in the synagogue at Capernaum about the Eucharist you were going to give to the world. You said, 'If you do not eat the flesh of the Son of Man and drink his blood, you will not have life in you. Anyone who does eat my flesh and

19

c

drink my blood has eternal life' (Jn 6:53f). And when many of your disciples left you because of this strange language, you let them go. Your body, broken, and your blood, poured out, were to become the sources of eternal life for us. In that sense, you on the cross are like the fruit of the tree of life, since the one who eats and drinks of it will live for ever.

And how useful to mankind this fruit is. In yielding your blood because your Father's will meant your death could not be avoided, you showed to all mankind, and to me, the way back into paradise. Your Father raised you from the dead, and showed you to the chosen witnesses, in such a way that at long last they understood your message of goodwill from God. We are to become like little children. We are to share your Father as our Father. He, and you, refused to lose patience even with your murderers; you forgave them instead. If we, like you, trust in our Father's love for us no matter what terrible trials we go through, and if we forgive our enemies, then we need not fear the sword of judgement. 'Judge not, and you shall not be judged', you have taught us (Mt 7:1). Human blindness was such that only your death and resurrection could open our eyes, to see that the flaming sword no longer bars our way through to paradise and the tree of life. And the fruit of this tree brings it about that you live in me and I live in you, as if my own tree were grafted on to yours, 'you the vine and we the branches' (cf. Jn 15:5). Although our eyes are veiled and we do not yet see clearly, already we sit in peace at your Father's table as your sisters and brothers.

What was lost, in the story of the eating of the forbidden fruit in Eden, is found again in a real way in this fruit of the tree of life. In Eden, Adam and Eve are pictured as having eaten of the knowledge of good and evil, because they wanted to be like gods. Now we are like gods: we are children of God and therefore sharers in the divine nature (cf. 2 Pt 1:4). Moreover, we have a 'knowledge of good' beyond our expectations: when someone in the gospel called you 'Good Master', you replied: 'Why do you call me good? One is good, namely God' (Mk 10:17). To know you, is to know good. If we are shoots grafted on to your tree, then our lives must follow the pattern of yours. We too become part of the tree of life for others. We must be prepared to yield up all we have if our Father so wishes, for the good of our sisters and brothers.

THE MASTER SPEAKS: You have no power of your own to live as I lived, no light of your own to find your way back to the tree of life. Pray always for the power to do what our Father wants of you. Be grateful always for the light you have been given to find your way to the Eucharist.

7

The holy vine of David

'We give thanks to you, our Father, for the holy vine of David your child, which you made known to us through Jesus your child; to you be glory for ever.' So runs a part of the Eucharistic Prayer spoken over the chalice, in the very early Christian document known as the *Didache*. The chalice is the holy vine of David. King David planned to build a temple in his new capital city of Jerusalem. 'Why should the Lord dwell in a tent,' he said, 'while I am in a rich house built of cedarwood? I will build a worthy house for the ark of the covenant.' The prophet Nathan replied for God, saying that on the contrary God would build a house for David, that is, a dynasty and long line of descendants to succeed to the throne, such that his would be an everlasting kingdom (cf. 2 Sam 7). The gospels make clear to us that Jesus is of the line of David, and that in him is fulfilled the promise made by God to David, since Christ in the resurrection is alive and will die no more, but will be King and Son of David for ever. The genealogies given by Matthew and Luke at the start of their gospels give the family tree from Abraham to Jesus (in Matthew) and from Adam to Jesus (in Luke), but both include the family tree of David leading to Jesus. In the book of *Revelation* Jesus is heard to say, 'I am of David's line, the root of David and the bright star of the morning' (Rev 22:16).

As we drink from the chalice, our adoption as children of God and brothers and sisters of Jesus is made, if possible, even clearer. In some sense we now share the royal blood of the family of David, and become sharers in the kingdom. As princes and princesses we are allowed, even encouraged, to think of the kingdom of heaven as our inheritance and our heritage: 'Father, in your mercy grant also to us, your children, to enter into our heavenly inheritance . . .' (Eucharistic Prayer IV).

In John's gospel at the Last Supper discourse, Jesus says, 'I am the vine, you are the branches'. He is at the heart of the family tree and the royal dynasty, but his apostles are branches. In this image it is rather the living sap which is the bond of life between the trunk and the branches. Jesus is very concerned that the apostles bear fruit by living always in him — fruit that will endure, fruit that will itself bear fruit in its turn (Jn 15:1–11).

Jesus is Son of God in his own right. We are sons and daughters of God by adoption, branches grafted on to Jesus' stock, always younger brothers and sisters to him the first-born.

In Mark's gospel, when Jesus enters Jerusalem as the Son of David, he looks for fruit on a tree, and finds none — it was not the season (Mk 11:13). Jesus when he comes to Jerusalem is like the son of the owner of the vineyard in his own parable. He is looking for fruit from the temple, on behalf of God the Father. The temple authorities were caught off guard, they were not ready; this was the wrong season for fruit. Like the stewards of the vineyard in Jesus' parable, they killed the Son and tried to keep all the future produce for themselves (Mk 12:1–9). In trying to destroy Jesus, the temple authorities actually set the scene for his own obedient sacrifice. He himself became the holy vine of David, which being divine could indeed be fruitful at all seasons of every year. He was the once-for-all sacrifice which rendered the temple with its many sacrifices useless from then onwards. The temple had become like the barren fruit tree, or like the thorns and thistles in Jesus' parables, useless because their growth was all show, without any fruit useful for human beings. No merely human temple could be always ready and fruitful.

The divine and royal Son, Jesus, was sent to invite mankind to join his royal family, to remain in him, to accept heaven as our inheritance, and give our obedience to God. Instead, he was killed, but the very killing made him the everlasting sacrifice, always fruitful and useful for us. In the shelter of this sacrifice all sins can be forgiven, even the sin of killing the king, and we can also bear lasting fruit ourselves, one vine, one stock with him. The holy vine of David offers its fruit to God by serving the needs of the hungry, the thirsty and the poor.

A prayer of loyalty

Jesus, Son of David, the crowds called you by that title as you entered Jerusalem, the city of David, in triumph (Mt 21:15). But within a week they were shouting, 'Crucify him! We have no king but Caesar'. Let me rather be like the blind man Bartimaeus, who called out to you, 'Jesus, Son of David, have mercy on me,' and when you heal my eyes let me follow you on your way no matter where you lead me (Mk 10:47). Let me acknowledge you as King of the Jews, and my king also. The assembled crowd of people from Judaea chose to release Barabbas and to have you crucified — 'Barabbas', 'son of his father', a name that implied he was illegitimate, and that no one knew his father's name. He was a rebel and a murderer (Mk 15:7). You are the only Son of God your Father, you are the obedient one, the holy and righteous one, the author of life (Acts 3:15). With all my heart I choose you as my king, and to you I promise my loyalty.

The soldiers clothed you in a purple cloak, then plaited a crown of thorns to put on your head. Then they mocked you and spat on you. Jesus, give me such strength in my loyalty that I would prefer to be sitting there being mocked along with you, wearing what you wear, rather than ever to join in the mockery. In your great goodness you have passed on to me your Father's invitation to become one of your royal family. Let me not expect to be treated any better than you were treated. Let me not expect to be crowned with any crown but yours, while there is anywhere in the world still hatred for your name. You deserved none of this cruel treatment. The same cannot be said of me. People mocked you even on the cross: 'He saved others; he cannot save himself. Let the Christ, the King of Israel, come down now from the cross, that we may see and believe' (Mk 15:32). Like a good vine, you gave up all your fruit as food and drink to be given free to the poor. You kept nothing for yourself. How proud I would be to share your epitaph: 'He saved others; he could not save himself'. You are my king, precisely because you did not come down from the cross, you did not try to escape when you could still have done so, in the garden of Gethsemane. You stayed there, so that even I would come to believe God wants me in his royal family.

You were God's only Son, come to Jerusalem to look for the

grapes and the wine of your Father's beloved vineyard, and at the end all that was offered you was a sponge full of vinegar, sour grapes (Is 5:4; Mk 15:36). In return you have given us this mystery of the Eucharist, which bears fruit for us at every season. Through this Eucharist may we always live in you, and you in us, so that our lives too may be fruitful. Teach us to be obedient to our Father's will, and not to go chasing dreams of our own that he never asked us to achieve. May our whole lives be such that we inspire those we know, to seek and find you. May we, as branches of your holy vine, not keep our fruits to ourselves but be ready to give them freely to those who hunger and thirst.

8

This is the cup of my blood

'When supper was ended, he took the cup. Again he gave you thanks and praise, gave the cup to his disciples, and said, "Take this, all of you, and drink from it. This is the cup of my blood ... " '. For those who spoke the Aramaic language Jesus spoke, the word for 'blood' meant far more than the word 'blood' means for us today. We have to imagine a person of that time and place who has received a wound which cannot be healed: as the blood flows from the body, so does the man's power of speech and his power of thinking, so does his very life leave his body. The blood and the life are linked in the mind of the one watching. The books of Moses in the Old Testament often repeat that no Israelite is ever to taste the blood of any creature, 'for the life of every creature is its blood' (cf. e.g., Lev 17:14). The blood, the life, belongs to God, and may be used only in sacrifices, never eaten or drunk in any form by human beings. When Jesus said first, 'This is my body' over the bread, and then, 'This is the cup of my blood' over the wine, he was clearly meaning his death; and he was asking the apostles to do something which sounded to them quite shocking, even more shocking than it sounds to us. No wonder many of the disciples stopped following him when he promised they would eat his flesh and drink his blood (Jn 6:66). But this gift of his body was to make them one body with him; this gift of his blood was to give them his life, his power of speech and his power of thinking, his spirit. And they have passed these wonderful gifts on to us. 'It is the spirit that gives life, the flesh is of no avail; the words that I have spoken to you are spirit and life' (Jn 6:23). These gifts are all things which belong to God alone, but they are given to us his children.

Probably it was the custom even in Jesus' time to mix some water with every cup of wine. In any case the Church has always understood the words 'This is my blood' to include both the divine and the human life of Jesus, the water as well as the blood. The Fathers of the Church tell us that in other forms of eating, what we eat and drink becomes what we are, is turned into us; but in the Eucharist we become what we eat and drink. So, we become one body, the body of Christ; so, we become one spirit, one life, the blood of Christ. Baptized and confirmed as children of God, we are fed and strengthened to grow in the likeness of Jesus his Son. The blood of the divine children, of the royal children, flows ever more strongly in our veins. The light of understanding comes to our minds; the power of speech comes to our tongues. The power of loyalty comes to our hearts, so that we can stay faithful under temptation and persecution. The body and blood we receive has been through death and risen again, so that is the pattern into which we grow. 'All the children share the same blood and flesh' (Heb 2:14); that is, Christ and we now share the same blood and flesh.

The Eucharist contains the seed of immortality. The Saviour gives up the blood from his body; the seed dies in the earth; the tree gives up its fruit. But this is the way of God, this is how much God loves us, this is the way God loves us. The death is not the end, for when Jesus died God raised him to a new life and showed him to the witnesses, so that we would know God's way is none other than the way Jesus taught us. The body and blood we receive is that of the risen Jesus; his body and blood will guide us along the way he went. Going by his way we too shall be fruitful, we too will die without need for fear. St Ignatius of Loyola came close to death three times after his 'conversion', so he tells us in his autobiography. In spite of his sinful past, he had no fear of death when death was staring him in the face, only a deep regret, that he had done so little in return, to thank his divine Majesty while he had the chance.

A prayer of thanksgiving to Jesus

Jesus, my life, how can I thank you enough for counting me in when you planned to reconcile mankind to your Father? The pessimist in me is always too ready to say about my human companions, 'Of course, they never thought about me, they left me out!' But whichever way we look at your marvellous work of saving us, we wonder at the way you left no one out of your heart. Those of us who are blessed with knowing you in our brothers and sisters and in your word and sacraments have so much more to thank you for. Would that we were generous enough to spend our lives making you better known and loved by the millions upon millions who have hardly ever heard of you.

Thank you for my parents, my family, my teachers. All of them, among countless other kindnesses they did me, with great love and gentleness taught me about your gift of yourself in the Eucharist, in such a way that I was never tempted to turn away and follow you no more. Thank you for the endless courtesy with which you have taken me as you found me, day after day, week after week, month after month, year after year. My presence to you in the Eucharist has been so forgetful or even boorish compared with your patient presence to me.

I thank you for your amazing unselfishness. You surely knew, from the first dawning of your mind and heart, God as your own Father (cf. Lk 2:49). You were able to see with clear eyes and an uncluttered heart that your Father wanted all mankind to share what you enjoyed. You must have spent years upon years composing your poems and parables and teachings in such a way that one day your disciples would be led to your Father. And you saw death, death for you, staring you in the face from the scriptures, but you still went steadily ahead. Who else but you would have gone to such pains, to hell and back indeed, all in order to give away your greatest treasure!

Forgive my ingratitude. Very often I receive the chalice of your blood and I am thinking, 'This will give me strength to do what I want to do'. Instead, I should be saying, 'This cost Jesus everything he had. May it give me strength enough to give myself away as he did'.

Were you conscious often of your blood, I wonder, once you knew you were going to lose it all on a cross? Our hearts are such quiet and efficient servants, we scarcely ever notice them except when we have been running or climbing, or when we are very afraid or excited. May we thank you for every drop of blood you shed for us, because you would not leave the least of us behind? For the blood you shed at your scourging, which we can scarcely bear to think of; for the blood you shed when your king's crown of thorns was put on your head; for the blood you shed on the way to

Golgotha, and for each of the five wounds we remember in our Easter liturgy and symbolize on our Easter candles: the wounds in your side. We thank you humbly for it all; and we thank you for your most precious treasure, the intimate knowledge which makes us daughters and sons of your Father.

9

Of the new covenant

'This is the cup of my blood, the blood of the new ... covenant.'
St Luke and St Paul change the words a little, 'This cup is the new
covenant in my blood'. There had been many covenants in the Old
Testament days. Since we call the scriptures written before Jesus
'The Old Testament', that is, the old covenant, we sometimes forget
that there was more than one covenant. In fact there were several:
there was, for instance, the covenant with Noah which we remember
when we see a rainbow; there were the covenants with Abraham in
which God promised to him the land his descendants would occupy,
and a great multitude of descendants to occupy it; there was another
promise to Isaac, and again to Jacob, that his descendants would
be as many as the specks of dust on the ground. Then came the
covenant we usually think of as the Old Covenant, the one with
Moses and the people at the giving of the Ten Commandments.
Last of all came the covenant with David, promising him an everlasting kingdom.

Most of these covenants or agreements were sealed with a
sacrifice, and the covenant with Moses involved the sprinkling of
the people with the blood of the sacrificed animal (Ex 24:8). In this
way the life of God (since all life belongs to God and is in his
image) was passed on to the people to give them strength and good
will to fulfil their part of the bargain. For sometimes, as at first
with Abraham and then with David, God promised what he promised and made no conditions; but the covenant sealed through
Moses involved very many and serious conditions. God would be
their God, if they would keep his laws, but not otherwise. In fact,
if they failed to keep his laws, he would punish them and bring
about their downfall.

As the centuries moved on towards the time in which Jesus was
born, there were two main sentiments gaining strength as regards
the covenant of Moses: either, and this is what the prophets were
beginning to say, 'God seems to be much more generous than even

his covenant with Moses suggested', or else, as the ancestors of the scribes and Pharisees were saying, 'We must redouble our efforts to keep all the laws perfectly, and have nothing to do with those who fail, since they are lost to God'.

It was the prophet Jeremiah who used the words quoted by Jesus about 'the new covenant': 'See, the days are coming — it is the Lord who speaks — when I will make a new covenant with the House of Israel . . . Deep within them I will plant my Law, writing it on their hearts . . . They will all know me, the least no less than the greatest, since I will forgive their iniquity and never call their sin to mind' (Jer 31:31–34).

In the New Covenant God says to each of us, 'I will be your Father; you will be my child'. The law is written in our hearts, because we all know how to respond to a loving father, even those of us who never had much love shown to them as children. We do not have to turn to anyone else and ask how to speak to God, once we know he has adopted us as his children.

Jesus was condemned to death on a charge, so far as the sanhedrin was concerned, of blasphemy. His blood sealed the new covenant, which for the followers of Jesus bypassed for ever the old covenant made through Moses.

A prayer of God's child

My Father, my lifegiver, I bless you for letting me live in the time of your new covenant. For many centuries people's eyes wanted to see what we have seen and their ears wanted to hear what we have heard through your beloved Son Jesus. The new covenant takes up into itself all the promises of the old covenants, and makes them rich beyond our dreams. Noah sent out a dove which returned to him as a sign of new life and the coming of a new springtime: to us you have given the dove of peace, the Spirit himself, and a new way of living even in our present world, as your own children. In the new covenant you have promised us eternal life, since we are children of you the ever-living God, and a land to dwell in, a promised land which we begin to see being created in our lifetime on earth and which will be ours in its fullness after death. We see the numbers of your family grow, so as nearly to equal the number of the stars in the heavens or the grains of sand in the desert. We see the laws of Moses replaced in our lives by your new commandment given us by your Son Jesus, a law guided by gratitude and love, no longer by fear. And we feel within our very selves the presence of your everlasting kingdom in which we are princes and princesses of the royal blood. How utterly simple is your new covenant: 'I will be your Father; you will be my child'. Yet none saw it, none dared to believe such a marvel, except perhaps little children who would be quickly educated out of such ideas, before you sent us your own Son Jesus.

Why were we so stubborn, that we could not believe his message as soon as he gave it? Where would I have stood, if I had been alive when first Jesus came to Jerusalem? Would I have had the courage to throw away the props and crutches of the law and to walk as a son of God should? If I had been a disciple, I would surely have run away as the others did, being afraid that Jesus might be wrong after all. He was on his own as he sealed the new covenant by his blood: in the lonely shedding of his life blood, he brought your life across the divide to us, with power to make us your children. He announced the new covenant in Galilee, then in Judaea and Jerusalem, day after day teaching in the temple. He was condemned for claiming to be your Son in a way no one else had ever made such a claim. The temple authorities could not bear to honour Jesus and to throw wide all the temple doors to the outcasts of the world simply because Jesus welcomed outcasts.

My Father, I honour Jesus and admit that he was and is your Son. He is the one who taught me to call you by the same name I always called my own father. Open wide the doors of my temple, of my heart and mind and body, to everyone that Jesus would welcome. Let me not criticize the temple at Jerusalem for shutting out so many people who hungered and thirsted for you, while I still shut out so many from my own heart.

Jesus, Redeemer, I thank you for giving your life-blood to seal the covenant by which we are God's children. Teach us always to treasure what you have won for us. May we always remember that we enjoy something which belonged first of all to you: you did not have to divide your inheritance with us, but at the sign of your Father's will you opened all your treasures to us. Praise and thanks to you, Jesus Son of God.

10

Of the everlasting covenant

'This is the cup of my blood, the blood of the new *and everlasting* covenant.' The old covenant between God on the one hand and Moses and the people on the other hand was a fragile affair. Many times the people of Israel broke their side of the bargain, and the covenant had to be made again and sealed again. But the new covenant brought by Jesus can never be broken: once a Father, always a Father, so far as God is concerned. No matter what we do to shake the agreement, God always keeps for us our own place at his table. Like the father of the Prodigal Son, our heavenly Father has forgiven our sins before ever we set out to commit them, and while we commit them, and always, into eternity.

The blood of Jesus has this to do with everlasting covenant: while Jesus shed his blood he was praying for his murderers, he was loving those who killed him. The resurrection of Jesus meant that the Father was blessing and ratifying all that Jesus had done in his name: so therefore the Father was saying: 'I forgive those who sin against me, as Jesus showed you. I love them still as my own children, as Jesus taught you and showed you'.

This knowledge in our hearts, that we are loved forever despite our own weakness and sinfulness, gives to the followers of Jesus an enormous freedom. 'We have our freedom through the shedding of his blood' (Eph 1:7). No longer do we have to justify our actions: we simply do our best to please God, and he is content. If we rail through weakness or even through malice, he will forgive us — he has already forgiven us. We do not serve for wages or in fear of punishment, but out of gratitude, trying to thank God for his great love shown first to us.

The reformer Martin Luther insisted that his followers stop the ancient custom of mixing a drop of water with the wine at the Eucharist. In his day the common Catholic understanding of the drop of water was that it represented our frail human efforts being added to the redeeming work of Christ. Luther would not have any suggestion that the work of Christ was somehow not enough. Well, as we have seen, there are other traditional ways of understanding the drop of water in the chalice. But what about the notion of our work being in some way added to that of Christ? For we have in these chapters used phrases like 'a share in his work', and 'Jesus wants us to bear fruit in him'. Do we share in the redeeming work or do we not? The answer is, surely, that any good actions of ours are only so because of the Spirit inspiring them. The freedom of heart which a Christian enjoys arises because his Father loves him whatever the outcome of his actions. Any action done under that influence is the work of the Spirit, not our work. The Christian is letting Christ take over his own body, so that Christ is using the Christian's eyes to see with, his ears to hear, his feet to take him where Christ wants to use his hands. Those who want to justify themselves do works of their own, but not a Christian. The saints and others who have helped us in our lifetime, bringing Christ to us, have done so only as mirrors reflecting the divine love. Any good we in our turn do, we do by passing on the freeing love that we have enjoyed from our Father through Jesus.

Because of this love which makes us free, the tree of life and the holy vine of David can be fruitful for ever. Only God can forgive sins, so the liberty in our hearts is divine, and being divine it will last forever. No power on earth can stop it growing.

Prayer of the freed captive

Father of mercy, I feel like your people in exile when they were set free to come back to Jerusalem: wanting to laugh and to sing, wanting to tell everyone the wonders you have done for me, and not only for me but for anyone who will trust your Son Jesus. Trying to save myself and earn heaven was such a slavery, such an exile of heart, working all hours for a master who gave me no thanks. But you took all my debts and tore them up at the start. Though I can never thank you enough, still I wish to thank you as much as I can, for as long as I live. I do not have to buy or earn your love — as if I could, as if anyone can ever earn the love of another!

34

Now I possess Jesus' greatest treasure: I may call you 'my Father'. And the treasure is mine for ever, not just as long as my behaviour seems to deserve the privilege. Remind me of your promised love, every hour of every day, so that I never slip back into the harsh anxiety of trying to come up to a standard I myself invented. Make of me a torch or a candle to be lit at your flame, so that your warm love can pass through me to others. Make me a fruitful branch of your beloved vine, so that others may taste in me your everlasting goodness. Take me over as your temple, and keep away from me all forms of competition: let me never compare my goodness with anyone else's, since all true goodness belongs to you and to none other. Let the only treasure in my heart always be that I may call you 'my Father' and that you call me your son. If that treasure fills my heart, and if I always remember the pain of my exile, then I will never be tempted to make anyone else pay for a share in my treasure. 'This poor man called, the Lord heard him and rescued him from all his distress' (Ps 33[34]: 6).

Jesus who set us free, I will always be in your debt for setting me free. I would dearly like to join forces with you now, and do what I can to help you pass your Good News of freedom on to others who are enslaved. By myself I can do nothing. Even if I toil away all night, like the apostles in their boat, I will catch nothing unless you show me where and how. Take over my body and my mind for your service; teach me to keep myself out of the way, to step back from myself and simply observe how you go about your work. If you want to go searching, use my eyes. Take my ears to listen patiently with, my mouth to speak your words. Take my feet to go wherever you choose; take my hands to labour for anyone you wish. I am sorry my skills are not greater, but your skill for your work is that of a master artist, so you can use even such a clumsy and blunt instrument as I am.

You have let me call you 'my brother'. All the more, then, you surely call me 'friend' as you called your apostles friends at the Last Supper. In that case, are you willing, my brother, to tell me all that you have learnt from our Father? (cf. Jn 15:15). Tell me at least what I need to know of the work you can do through me, so that I can try not to get in the way. Or if it would be better that I know nothing, because I would only hinder the work, then please keep me in the dark. But do work through me, as you worked through those many, many servants of yours who brought to me your key of freedom.

11

It will be shed for you and for all

Jesus at the Last Supper talks about the future: this blood will be shed 'for you and for all'. The old English translation was 'for you and for many', but Greek words in the New Testament are an idiom and mean 'for you and *for all*'. Here is one of the most startling differences between the new covenant and all previous covenants. Always in the past the covenants were between God and a leader of the people, or between God and all the people of Israel. This one is between God and everybody, everywhere. There was no belief in an after-life among the Jews until a couple of centuries before Christ, and even in his time only a section of the people believed in life after death; so 'salvation' was a matter of physical peace and prosperity, riches, a large family, freedom from sickness, freedom of worship, and such-like good things of this life. We need not think of the Jews happily making a covenant with God about everlasting life, from which they excluded most of the inhabitants of the world. The coming of a belief in life after death was another reason why there needed to be a new covenant. There seems to be good reason for thinking Jesus would have worked through the temple and the Jewish authorities if they had made him welcome: he only bypassed them when they reacted with anger to all his teachings and actions and suggestions. Even the Pharisees, who did believe in a life after death, bridled at Jesus' concern for all the 'wrong' people.

Jesus welcomed women as readily as men, little children, the poor, the blind, the deaf, the dumb, the paralysed, epileptics, lepers; he welcomed sinners like the tax-collectors and prostitutes, as well as Samaritans, Romans and Greek-speakers from around the Mediterranean. The tax-collectors were regarded as traitors. The Romans were the hated oppressors of the Jewish nation. Jesus spoke well of people in prison, identifying himself with them long before he joined their company. The city of God would have nothing to do with this sort of broadcast love; it threw Jesus out and killed him outside the walls. To put the same idea in poetic language, the city of Jerusalem, which should have have been the bride of God, threw out the word or the seed of God, but the seed grew and bore fruit outside the walls, free now of the narrowness of the city's limits. If the city had excluded even one poor wretch from its welcome (for instance, if it had excluded me), surely Jesus would have let himself be thrown outside and be killed rather than desert that one.

Such, then, is the kind of love to which the blood of Christ is always urging us. Those who are conscious of being on the way to God's salvation are expected by Jesus to show his courtesy and welcome to all, especially the poor, the sick and the outcasts of our own society. We had better be prepared, since in the after-life they will all be there in the new Jerusalem, and Jesus having given his blood and his life to get them there is not going to remove any of them to suit my whim. Would-be citizens of the new Jerusalem must be readier than those of the old Jerusalem to open the gates to all the wrong people. However, that same readiness brings its own rewards even now. As Jesus observed, the wrong people often have far more to teach us about God's ways than the right people, and being with them expands the heart and its capacity for joy.

Prayer for a wide heart

Jesus, my friend, St Paul tells us that through you God was pleased to reconcile to himself all things, whether on earth or in heaven, making peace by the blood of your cross (cf. Col 1:19f). Paul makes it sound as if you have reconciled again the birds and the animals and the trees to God, and all the things as well as all the people of earth. Poor creatures, that they were ever involved in our sin, which veiled our eyes so that even the beauty of your world was dimmed for a time. You cared about the sparrows, you watched with a poet's eye all the world of the farmer as well as the worlds of the villager and the city-dweller. Thank you for caring about us, with your heart so wide it spanned the centuries as well as the miles. You gave your blood for us all, so please have a special care for all those I love, and all those who love me. Sad to say, they are not always the same people, 'those I love' and 'those who love me'. Usually they are the same, but sometimes the love is stronger on one side than on the other.

You, I am sure, know all about that, since you have loved us so long with so little return of love from us. Take care especially of all those of my friends who are less than completely respectable. May I be counted worthy of their company in heaven. Give me a sympathy as wide as yours, to carry in my heart all the outcasts of the world today. I gave you already my eyes, my ears, my mouth, my hands and my feet. Take my heart now, and use it as your own. I am such a lover of routine, at times even one unexpected visitor at the table can put me out of sorts. However will I cope with having a heart like yours! You must widen and warm my heart, since left to itself it always grows cold and narrow.

Father of all, Jesus tells us that not even one sparrow falls to the ground without your knowing about it. How hard they work, the sparrows and all small birds, finding food, bringing up their nestlings, watching out for danger, surviving the winter. When we watch them, as Jesus told us to (Mt 6:26), we can see that of course you follow their every movement and care for the outcome. What, then, about your people, the crown of your creation by design? Do you not follow every action of ours with immense love, even or especially when we take ourselves into danger? I have asked Jesus to take my heart as his own, but if for any reason that is impossible, then let me at least give a full and loving attention to those I meet in my own narrow world. If I cannot love everyone in the world, let me love those who are in my world. Give me courtesy and interest for the strangers, especially, since I often have contact with strangers. Each of them is as lovable as my dearest friends, or so at least you think. Each of them is as lovable as I am. Why should I dare to write them off quickly as too much trouble, when you love each one of them as much as you love me?

I pray for reconciliation everywhere: between nation and nation, between religion and religion, between Christian and Christian. I pray for justice and peace between the rich and the poor. I pray that we may all see your beloved image in the faces of all our sisters and brothers. In your heaven we will all have to get along together and love one another. There is so little time to prepare.

12

So that sins may be forgiven

A great building or a great city is built upon the body and blood of Christ, but the foundation is the forgiveness of our sins. Unless our sins are forgiven, the work of Christ cannot go any further. Our forgiveness was not the sole purpose of Jesus' saving work, but it was the beginning. 'In him we have redemption through his blood, the forgiveness of our sins' (Eph 1:7). Once we are forgiven and our hearts set free, then we can begin to look for and fulfil our Father's wishes for us. The work of our forgiveness was announced by Jesus from the start of his public life, but it was only complete when he died and shed the last drop of his blood for us. 'This is my blood, the blood of the covenant, which is to be poured out for many for the forgiveness of sins' (Mt 26:28).

Our sins are forgiven because we are children of God, under the new covenant. A loving father and mother will always forgive the sins of their children: once our wrongdoing is put on that footing, as something to be settled between parent and child and not any longer a matter for judgement and the law courts, then our sins are forgiven for ever, from the first moment we were conceived. If we are estranged from God or ashamed of the things we have done, then we are invited by the Gospel to go like the Prodigal Son and say, 'Father, I have sinned against you', and we will find forgiveness (cf. Lk 15:21).

The blood of Jesus is involved for two reasons. First, Jesus was killed for announcing the Good News that God is our Father and that therefore our sins are forgiven. In Jesus' resurrection God was seen to be vindicating the teachings of Jesus: so the covenant and the forgiveness of sins were realities and not idle dreams. Secondly, Jesus was not only teaching about God's mercy, he was demonstrating it by his actions. He who had said, 'To have seen me, Philip, is to have seen the Father' (cf. Jn 14:9), was praying for his murderers even as they were killing him. Once again, in the resurrection God was agreeing with Jesus, as much as to say, 'Here is my Son: look at him if you wish to know me'. There could have been no such resurrection for one who gave a false picture of God. In the Eucharist the blood of Jesus is an everlasting reminder to God (and, more importantly, to ourselves who so often forget it) of his great mercy that was shown to us in the death and resurrection of Jesus.

Jesus forgave those who sinned against him, and to that extent we can all forgive sins, namely the sins committed against ourselves personally. Apart from forgiving those who sinned against himself, Jesus only said to the others, 'Your sins are forgiven', that is to say, 'God has forgiven your sins'. Again, that is something any of us can say truly to any other person, since God is our Father and has already from all eternity forgiven us — though not all sinners would want to or be ready to hear those words, so we would have to be very careful. Jesus did not say, 'I forgive your sins against God', but, to the paralytic, 'Son, your sins are forgiven', to the woman who was a sinner, 'Your sins are forgiven', and to all, 'Forgive, and you will be forgiven'.

The forgiveness of God is there if we only wish for it and ask for it. After that, we must extend our own forgiveness to those who offend us, and to those who offend God. 'Do not judge, and you will not be judged yourselves' (Lk 6:37) is a true saying and a safe guideline only because of the blood of Jesus. His teaching on judgement and forgiveness is so lenient and beautiful we would never have dared to believe it but for his death and resurrection.

Prayer of a sinner

Father of kindness, which of us would have dared to think of you so lovingly had it not been for Jesus whom you gave to us? On the day you took me for your child, which was not just the day of my baptism but 'before the foundation of the world' when 'you chose us in Christ' (Eph 1:4), you were already determined to love each of us no matter how we turned out. In my life you are to me like a net of safety below me and an inspiration above me, telling me always not to worry about yesterday but to walk bravely onwards and upwards to where you are calling. Make me know ever more deeply the free-

dom that comes from your covenant with me. I get so tangled up by
the foolish or downright wicked things I did yesterday, when all the
time you have forgotten yesterday, and it is only my own disgust I
mistake for yours.

Thank you also for the Sacrament of Reconciliation, by which
your Church brings the power of the blood of Christ to bear upon the
sins we still commit in spite of our Baptism — a sacrament in which
I have found so much peace. We celebrate in your Church the forgiveness you have already granted, and we can return as many times
as we wish to where you, our dear Father, wait for your children, to
welcome them.

Jesus, my elder brother, you are not like the elder brother of the
Prodigal Son in your parable (Lk 15). He was resentful of the fuss
his father made over the younger brother returned home. You are
so much of one mind with your heavenly Father, you were often to
be found eating and drinking and celebrating with your younger
sisters and brothers returned to God after a sinful life. You went out
and searched for the prodigal sons and daughters in the highways
and byways, and brought them home like a shepherd gathering in the
lost sheep.

So single-minded and determined were you to safeguard the total
forgiveness of your Father, that you called 'wolves' those who judged
and condemned others, spreading alarm and fear by their false notion
of God and scattering his flock. They said yours was the false notion.
'Father, forgive them', you prayed from the cross, 'they do not know
what they are doing' (Lk 23:34). I pray with you, that one day, the
wolf may live with the lamb (Is 11:6)). I too have suffered torment,
years of torment, because people put a false mask over the face of
your Father. I join with you in asking him to forgive them. They were
well intentioned, for all they were blind guides. Ask pardon for me,
too, since I was blind myself, even when I was called to be a shepherd
in your name.

I forgive now and always those who have done me any kind of
harm in the past; some will have harmed me on purpose, and many
more have done so without realizing. I pray for them by name . . . and
for those I have hurt in the past, often without knowing it, and who
perhaps pray for me because I was like an enemy to them.

I am consoled when I recall how gently you make the father of the prodigal speak to the elder son, the 'Pharisee' son, after his refusal to join his brother's feast. The story ends, and still the father leaves the door open (Lk 15:32).

And when it comes to working for your kingdom, or any of my daily tasks and duties, let me not give all my service and attention only to those who are rich or talented or well-disposed. Give me your instinct for the lost sheep and the lonely and the ones we call 'God-forsaken'. Our Father has not forsaken them at all, but perhaps I, his messenger, have. So many of them are just waiting for a word of encouragement, while I stay on well-trodden paths and never find them.

13

The leaves for healing

The prophet Ezekiel describes a vision of a river that had its source under the temple and which grew into a mighty stream. On either bank of the river grew trees. 'Their leaves will not wither nor their fruit fail, but they will bear fresh fruit every month, because the water for them flows from the sanctuary. Their fruit will be for food, and their leaves for healing' (Ezek 47:12). These trees reappear as the trees of life or the tree of life in the *Revelation* to John, in the description of the holy city, the new Jerusalem: 'also, on either side of the river, the tree of life with its twelve kinds of fruit, yielding its fruit each month; and the leaves of the tree were for the healing of the nations' (Rev 22:2). We have compared the Eucharist to the tree of life, and the likeness may be seen also in the 'leaves of the tree for the healing of the nations', since the Eucharist is not simply food and drink but also a power for healing, not just food for the present and future but a healing of the scars and wounds of the past. We believe that there is only one sacrifice, and that is the offering of himself to the Father by Jesus, for the forgiveness of our sins. The cross which held the body and blood of Jesus is the same as the tree of life with its fruit present in the Eucharist in a timeless moment. All power of reconciliation and pardon comes from that one sacrifice. We have in the past often overlooked the power of the Eucharist itself to bring us the forgiveness of our sins. As we come together for the Eucharist, we remember Jesus' warning: 'So if you are offering your gift at the altar, and there remember that your brother has something against you, leave your gift there before the altar and go; first be reconciled to your brother, and then come and offer your gift' (Mt 5:23f). We remember that we are not to condemn, so as not to be condemned ourselves. We acknowledge our own sins, and ask forgiveness of God and of one another. Then the celebrant prays for our pardon.

In the Eucharistic Prayers, the same sacrifice of Christ is offered to the Father, with ourselves like chickens under the wing of the mother-hen, seeking shelter, pardon and other gifts. At the time of communion, we pray to Jesus as Lamb of God to have mercy on us; the priest prays to him, 'By your holy body and blood free me from all my sins and from every evil'; or again, 'Lord Jesus Christ, with faith in your love and mercy I eat your body and drink your blood. Let it not bring me condemnation, but health in mind and body'. Then everybody says, '. . . only say the word and I shall be healed'. After the communion the priest's prayer runs: 'May these gifts bring me healing and strength, now and forever'.

Wine of itself has the power of healing, according to the New Testament. Timothy is advised to 'have a little wine for the sake of your stomach and your frequent ailments' (1 Tim 5:23); and the Good Samaritan in the parable poured oil and wine on the wounds of the man who fell into the hands of bandits, before putting bandages on the wounds (Lk 10:34).

Perhaps the most startling of all prayers for forgiveness comes in the first Eucharistic Prayer, the Roman Canon. A literal translation from the Latin, of the prayer that begins 'For ourselves, too . . .' would run: 'And to us sinners, your servants, hoping in the multitude of your mercies, be pleased to grant some share and company with your holy apostles and martyrs . . . and with all your saints. Please admit us into their number, not as a measurer of our merit, but as a generous giver-out of forgiveness'.

Jesus speaks with the traveller

JESUS, GOOD SAMARITAN, SPEAKS: I found you lying by the road, with no one to care for you. I saw how others passed you by, walking deliberately on the other side of the road so as not to get themselves involved with you. But you were, after all, my brother, my younger brother, so there was no question of my passing you by, even though the cut-throats might still be somewhere around. Better for both of us to die, robbed of every penny, than for one of us to leave the other behind, don't you agree? So I gave you some wine to drink, just a little, as I raised up your head and began to find out how badly you were hurt. My poor brother, your wounds were bad, and you had been left to lie there too long, so I tore up some bandages from some clean linen I had with me, but first I poured oil and wine on your wounds to stop them festering. The next thing was to get you on my beast somehow and to stop you from falling off as we made our way to the inn. Once we got there it was easy, I could look after you properly. They are used to such strange guests in that inn, and they do not ask too many questions. But their hearts are good, and I could trust them far enough the next day to leave them some money to see to your needs. Just to be on the safe side, I reminded them that I would be coming back that way soon and would call in to see how you were.

THE TRAVELLER SPEAKS: When did all this happen, my brother, and when did you save my life?

JESUS REPLIES: You were dazed at the time, and hardly conscious. But it did happen, and I would do the same again for you, and more besides. Now that you are better and stronger, walk bravely along the road you must follow, and remember that I myself walk all roads. I will be with you to heal you, if you should fall again into the hands of robbers.

THE TRAVELLER: What a comfort it is to me, to know that you were aware of my danger even before I knew it myself, and that you will continue to keep guard over my ways. To me each eucharistic celebration I attend is itself like a visit to that inn. You are the silent, unseen healer, and to you I can show the scars and wounds and sores of my journey, for you to heal with your soothing oil and wine. Then you cheer my heart with the bread and wine of the Eucharist which you have paid for, and give me strength to face out upon the road again. You heal me with your own life-blood, because each time I am in its presence and each time I drink from the chalice I am reminded of how much you are willing to put up with and forgive in me. Almost we could say, you died for us because there was no other way we would believe you really loved us as a brother. If ever I find myself again unable to reach the inn, lying half-dead by the roadside, then will you please come and find me once again, and bring me the comfort that only you can bring?

14

The acceptable sacrifice

Mankind was offering sacrifices to gods long before Abraham 'our father in faith' came to offer sacrifice to our God, whom we now know as our Father. The instinct of sacrifice seems to have faded nowadays in the human heart, perhaps partly because of the Christian religion: we no longer *miss* the experience of killing animals or burning crops to keep on the right side of our gods. Yet for centuries upon centuries this was a deadly serious business, for if the gods were not appeased then the crops might fail, wars could be lost, children could sicken . . . The sacrifice said to the god or goddess of a place: 'All we have is your gift. We take the most precious of your gifts and give them back to you in the only way we know how. See, we are your humble servants. Take our side, please, against all our enemies; give us prosperity so that your name will be respected'.

Since the blood of Jesus was shed, his followers have used no other sacrifice. In his death and resurrection we knew for ever that the one and only God is our own intimate Father, a Father, to each one of us as if he had no other children. So what possible need could there be of sacrifice any more? For a few years the early Christians still out of force of habit went to the temple in Jerusalem, but soon they had worked it out that Jesus himself was all that God would ever ask for by way of sacrifice. The reason the language of the New Testament is so heavily laden with references to sacrifice, and the language of Christian liturgy as well, is surely that the writers of the New Testament were all brought up in a world where sacrifices were terribly important, whether one was a Jew or a pagan; so to give up offering them was a shock, and replacing them with Baptism and the Eucharist had to be justified in terms of sacrifice. Jesus himself prepared the way by the words in which he spoke of the death he was to suffer: 'and when I am lifted up', and 'my blood of the covenant', and so on. The arguments of, say, the *Letter to the Hebrews* are very beautiful and very convincing, but there is a mental effort for us today in trying to think ourselves back into a world where sacrifices of animals and farm produce were taken for granted.

Jesus was the priest and the victim. He offered himself to do the will of his Father: 'In the head of the book it stands written, that I should do your will' (Ps 39[40]:8). 'You asked no holocaust or sacrifice for sin; then I said, "Here I am! I am coming!" ' (*ibid*, v. 7). Our Father's will was for Jesus to offer mankind a new covenant, a covenant of adoption. The day came when Jesus had to choose between saving his life and completing his task: he chose to persevere, and was killed. His blood was shed from his body. His sacrifice was accepted by God his Father: Jesus was lifted up on the cross and lifted up into glory, and all his prayers as our priest were answered. The covenant was sealed, and in the Eucharist he had left behind he gave us the atonement of our lives and a communion with his own body and blood, so that we are carried with him into the presence of the Most High God, but without fear. 'This blood I myself have given you to perform the rite of atonement for your lives at the altar' (Lev 17:11). 'The blessing-cup that we bless is a communion with the blood of Christ, and the bread that we break is a communion with the body of Christ' (1 Cor 10:16). 'There is one Body, one Spirit' (Eph 4:4). Jesus was 'like a trustful lamb being led to the slaughter-house' (Jer 11:19), knowing full well what was in store for him, but determined to bring back pardon even for his murderers.

A prayer of submission

Father of peace, we have been welcomed into your presence through the blood of Jesus your Son, our Lord. We can see now that your intentions towards us were never hostile; it was our darkened and guilty hearts which did not dare to believe in your goodness. All your messengers to us we killed, refusing to listen to them, blocking our ears in case they should tell us the truth about ourselves. Even your beloved Son could not live long in our company, before we killed him as well. But this time we had met our match. His goodness was even greater than our malice. We killed him, but his death and resurrection became a sacrifice on our behalf, and the truth he told us about ourselves was that we are your children,

48

brothers and sisters to himself. When the crowds cried out to Pilate, 'His blood be on us and on our children' (Mt 27:25), he took it as a prayer and not a curse, and gave up his blood as if to be sprinkled over them, to seal the new covenant and to give them strength to do your will. The high priest in the sanhedrin complained sometime later that the apostles were trying to 'bring this man's blood upon us' (Acts 5:28) and indeed they were, but not in order to accuse, rather to bring your mercy and forgiveness to your chosen people.

Sacrifice may be a strange notion to us in our time, but we still use the word 'sacrifice', and the way we use it is close to the meaning your Son gave to his own sacrifice. We know what it is to sacrifice our own will for the sake of something we consider greater than ourselves. Sometimes our sacrifices are foolish, because we give up our lives for a cause that involves human glory but has little to do with your will. Sometimes we are in love with sacrifice, and do anything rather than our own will, and that too can be foolish : as often as not your will is that we make up our own minds and do what we decide for the best (Lk 12:57), so why should we be afraid of our own decisions about our own lives, choosing someone else's decisions instead?

But first we must pray, as Jesus prayed so often when he was looking to find your will, or when he was looking for strength to do what he already knew was your will. Father, I want to join the sacrifice of my life to Jesus' sacrifice of his life. We Christians now are called to be one body, one spirit, his body and his spirit in our world today. If your Son is to be seen and heard it must be through us, and by your power. Nothing we do now can add to his sacrifice or subtract from it, but we can either obscure it or proclaim it. We have no power in ourselves to do your will, to take your chalice and accept wholeheartedly the life that you send us. If our lives and our death can be joined to his in proclaiming the Good News, then the glory is all yours.

May my life be given over, as Jesus' life was, to making known your tremendous love for us. May I speak of it in my words, and show it in my actions. Neither of these can I do unless you give me the power. I can pick up the chalice and drink from it at the Eucharist, but that means nothing unless you inspire me by it to follow your call. I can look and look again at the world around me, and not see what the body and blood of Christ is urging me to do, unless you and he open my eyes. And then I can do nothing unless you empower me. All the ailments to be found in the gospel seem to be found in me: I am by turns blind, deaf, dumb, paralysed, fevered, and a leper in my own eyes, though not in yours. Whether or not I see for myself what is happening, use my life to bring others to love you. I do not ask to give my blood as Jesus did, because I could not bear to look forward to a martyrdom. But whatever way death comes to me, let it be at the end of a life given over to your will, and in a way that shows I am returning gladly to you.

15

The sacrifice of Abraham

In the first Eucharistic Prayer after the consecration the following prayer is included: 'Look with favour on these offerings and accept them as once you accepted the gifts of your servant Abel, the sacrifice of Abraham, our father in faith, and the bread and wine offered by your priest Melchizedek'. At first sight the prayer seems to be upside down. Here in the Mass we have the sacrifice of Christ offering himself on the cross, and our own offering of ourselves (chicks under the mother-hen's wings, sheep for whom the shepherd died). Of course the sacrifice of Christ will always be looked on with favour by God, infinitely more so than even the sacrifices of Abel, Abraham or Melchizedek. There would still seem to be two good reasons for including the prayer: one, to pray that our dispositions may be such that we can be united to the sacrifice of Christ, because we sincerely want God's mercy and we are trying to be merciful to others, and secondly because the comparisons between Christ's sacrifice and these three Old Testament sacrifices are helpful to our own understanding of the Mass.

The story of Cain and Abel is told in chapter four of *Genesis*. Abel was a shepherd and a Cain a farmer. They both offered sacrifice to God, Abel bringing the first-born of his flock and some of their fat as well, Cain bringing some farm produce. God was pleased with Abel's sacrifice, but not with Cain's: no clear reason is given, except that there seems to be something wrong with Cain's dispositions. Perhaps there was already jealousy and murder in his heart. Be that as it may, Cain killed Abel, so Abel's sacrifice became his own self. He died, an innocent victim, simply because he was pleasing to God. So runs the story.

Abraham was willing to sacrifice his only son Isaac, because he thought that was what God wanted (Gen 22). The sacrifice of children was not unknown in that part of the world in his day, and the horrific

51

practice still survived many centuries later. The story of how Jephthah killed his daughter to fulfil a vow he had made to God is a poignant reminder of this fact (Judg 11:29–40). Presumably Abraham first thought God wanted the sacrifice of Isaac, and then at the crucial moment his mind became clear that God could want no such thing. He had, however, been willing to make the sacrifice when he thought that was what God wanted. In this sense we can still keep the main lines of the story in *Genesis*, that God 'put Abraham to the test', and that Abraham passed the test. Very often in our own lives we can for quite a time make some sacrifice which costs us a lot in pain or inconvenience, until one day it dawns on us that our sacrifice is uncalled-for, so we stop. We have however shown God we were willing to make the sacrifice, and that therefore we would do as much again should he ask it of us.

Melchizedek is mentioned briefly and mysteriously in the story of Abraham. He was the king of Salem and he came to meet Abraham, bringing 'bread and wine; he was a priest of God Most High', and Abraham gave him tithes of his belongings, as if Melchizedek had a right to them (Gen 14:18). Melchizedek seems to have been a conciliator after some local wars. After that he is never mentioned again, except in one of the psalms: 'The Lord has sworn an oath he will not change, "You are a priest for ever, a priest like Melchizedek of old" ' (Ps 109[110]:4). And in Christian times, the *Letter to the Hebrews* mentions him a few times to make comparisons with Jesus as high priest. Because Melchizedek's birth and death are not recorded in *Genesis*, the author of *Hebrews* compares him to Jesus the Son of God, 'whose life has no beginning or ending. He remains a priest for ever' (Heb 7:3):

Prayer to the Son and to the Father

Jesus, you were the innocent victim of all our human quarrels and hatreds. You tried to teach us your way to God, but no one would listen. In the end it was only in your death that you managed to convince a few. You loved us right to death and beyond. Nothing could make you hate us in return for what men did to you. And today, nothing can make you hate us in return for what we stlll do to you. In the words of scripture, Abel's blood cried out to God from the ground. It cried out for vengeance, because it was innocent blood and Cain had shed it. But your blood cries out even more insistently to God to be merciful to us (Heb 12:24). How much more kindly is your new covenant than the old! Open my ears to hear your blood crying out to your Father in a prayer that will most surely be answered, pleading for forgiveness for me and for all people.

We read, Jesus, that Isaac was his father Abraham's only son. All the promises made to Abraham, about his countless descendants who would inherit the land, depended upon this one boy who was none the less being offered in sacrifice by him in response to the supposed wishes of God your Father. The promises of the new covenant depended in a similar way upon you, my Lord Jesus. There was to be a new Israel, a new Jerusalem, a kingdom as wide as the world, a fruitful new vine with spreading branches, a new shepherd for a new and numberless flock, and all these promises and more depended upon you. Yet to human eyes, at the end of your short career as a prophet and preacher you seemed a failure. On the cross you cried out with the psalmist, 'My God, my God, why have you forsaken me?' Surely that cry was genuine, straight from your heart, so you must have felt yourself to be a failure in that blackest of black moments. You had wanted to create the new Israel out of the old, you had come to the old Jerusalem to give her the chance to become new, and now you were cast out, cast out of the city, cast out of the vineyard, and in deadly pain on the cross. Isaac carried the wood for his own sacrifice up the hill; you too, my Jesus, carried the wood on which you were to die up the hill of Golgotha. The sacrifice of Isaac was halted at the last moment, but there was to be no halting of your sacrifice. In my moments of black darkness, remind me how a new and everlasting kingdom arose out of those ruins of your life.

Lord Jesus, high priest of the line of Melchizedek, making peace between God and men, I wonder at your choosing bread and wine, just those two, for the offerings at your Last Supper. For two thousand years, between Melchizedek and yourself, nobody seems to have made an offering of just those two: bread from the earth and wine for inspiration, this your body and that your blood. I wonder at the simplicity of your gestures and words, which yet conceal such depths of wisdom and knowledge. I could have puzzled a thousand years over the scriptures of the old covenant and never have guessed that you would take bread and wine to perpetuate your sacrifice; yet once you do it, how obvious the choice seems. Praise to you, Lord Jesus Christ! Praise for evermore!

Dearest Father, when the story of Abraham and Isaac has been taken by Christians and given a new meaning, then Jesus your Son is cast in the role of Isaac, and you yourself are given the part of Abraham — Abraham who was willing to sacrifice his own son if needs must. But the comparison falls down in so many respects. You wanted the safety and rescue of all humankind. Your Son was destined by you to teach us the way of salvation, the way of accepting your adoption of ourselves as your children. His death was surely not planned or wanted by you. We gave him his death. Isaac was saved from death; your Son Jesus had no one to save him from death. The men who held the nails and the lance for his execution were in no frame of mind to listen to what you were saying to them, as Abraham had listened and then put down his knife; so the execution went ahead. He was your Son. 'Can he who made the eye, not see?' (Ps 93[94]:9). And can he who made the heart, not feel? You must have felt all the anguish of Abraham, and how many times more? All the sorrow of Jephthah, and how many times more? I remember the father of a little boy who was burnt in an accident telling me that nobody could imagine his pain as a parent without having experienced it. Feel again for me, my Father, feel for all your children in the hour of our death. Turn death's victory into your victory, through Jesus who died for us. Amen.

16

The two great commandments

When Jesus was asked, what was the greatest commandment of the Law, he answered that the first and greatest of all is to love God with all our heart; the second is to love our neighbour as much as we love ourselves (cf. Mk 12 : 28–31). It is not immediately clear what the first commandment entails: worship and attending the synagogue or the temple ceremonies, perhaps, and speaking well of God and keeping the Sabbath? Yet Jesus and the great prophets before him always insist that these in themselves are no use without works of kindness, especially towards the poor and downtrodden. Maybe the heart of the first great commandment, in Jesus' thought about it, lies in accepting God's fatherly love and forgiveness; then the second commandment asks that we pass on the same love and forgiveness to others. In that way worship in church or synagogue is an expression of something in our hearts, rather than an end in itself. 'As the Father has loved me, so have I loved you' (Jn 15:9), said Jesus, showing that his own life was a reflection of love already given him by the Father. Then he turns to his disciples and says, 'As I have loved you, so love one another' (Jn 13 : 34). In other words, they are to look at the way the Father has loved them in Jesus, and then reflect that same love to all other people.

Thus the first commandment is faith: to believe in God's love and forgiveness. The second is love: to love others and forgive them as we have been loved and forgiven. And it seems reasonable to connect the first command of faith with the bread of life in the Eucharist, and the second commandment of love with the chalice.

We have already prayed about the bread of life as 'the bread of the children'. Especially if we include the drop of water which is mingled with the wine in the chalice, then the bread and water of the Eucharist speaks to us of God's love and forgiveness for each one of us, his gift to us of adoption as his children, his daily providence, and all his gifts of body and mind to each one, and the presence of Christ as our brother. Our response to the body of Christ when we receive it is mainly an act of faith: 'I believe that God is my loving Father, through Jesus Christ who is here with me, and who has opened my ears to hear, my eyes to see, and my lips to praise'.

The chalice, on the other hand, in which the drop of water is mixed, speaks more about our response of love and action. As God has loved me in Christ, so it is my desire to love and serve and forgive all others. I take the chalice to be united more closely to the divine life of Christ, without which I cannot hope to love and forgive others as I should.

St Ignatius of Antioch, writing about the year 106 A.D., uses similar language about faith and love, the body and blood of Christ: 'Renew yourselves in faith, which is the flesh of the Lord, and in love, which is the blood of Jesus Christ' (*To the Trallians* 8:1). And again, 'Bread of God is what I desire; that is, the flesh of Jesus Christ, who was of the seed of David; and for my drink I desire his blood, that is, incorruptible love' (*To the Romans* 7:3). 'Here is the beginning and the end of life: faith is the beginning, the end is love; and when these two blend perfectly with each other, they are God' (*To the Ephesians* 14:1).

When the Father loves me and I gladly receive his love, then the Spirit comes from the Father to me. When I, knowing I am loved, try to love others as the Father has loved me, then the Spirit comes from the Son in me.

A prayer for faith and love

Blessed Virgin Mary, your vision was so clear and your humility so great, you almost sound as if you were boasting in your song of praise: 'From now on all generations will call me blessed'. But then we read on and you tell us why they will call you blessed: 'For he who is mighty has done great things for me' (Lk 1:48f). All your goodness, all your strength was a reflection of the good God who is our Father. If he had not loved you first, you alone could have done nothing: if his light had not shone first, your mirror would have been only dark. Help me, please, to count all the blessings our good Father has lavished on me, and to believe that they all come from him with everlasting love, because he is my Father. Help me especially to remember his goodness when I receive from his table the bread of life, the body of Christ my Lord, your Son. United with Jesus, may I then take the chalice as a thanksgiving, so my heart may be flooded with love for my friends, and for the poor, the hungry and the thirsty, and even for my enemies. Please ask all these gifts for me from your Son Jesus.

Ever living, ever loving Father, grant us the grace to love one another as you have loved us first. I thank you for my parents and my family, and all the love they have shown me year after year; for my friends and for my teachers, and for all the wealth of people I have met more briefly.* Thank you for your love shown to me through them, and for 'the wonder of my being' and all the riches of nature. Thank you above all for calling me your child and inviting me to your table. The divine bread which I eat there nourishes me with your love. The water I drink whispers still, as it did in the stream, that your love for me is never ending. And the chalice of wine — please may it transform me, so that when I take it I can begin to thank you. I sit there at the table, and I am like the man in Jesus' parable who had a debt of ten thousand talents completely cancelled (Mt 18:23). For how could I ever repay you for my life? How could I repay you for becoming my Father? My debt is beyond any repayment in money. But unless you give me yet another gift, the gift of forgiving others, I will be no better than that unforgiving debtor in the parable. The blood of your Son cried out to you to forgive his enemies. When I drink it, make my heart and mind forgive everyone as he did.

* The reader will bear in mind, in this and similar prayers, that the writer is a Jesuit, and therefore unmarried. Married readers will naturally wish to add thanks to God for their life's partner, and for each of their children by name.

17

Not made by human hands

In the offertory prayers at Mass the priest says a prayer blessing God for 'this bread ... which earth has given and human hands have made'. In the scriptures and the early Fathers of the Church we find the description 'made by human hands' given to many things which are earthly and earth-bound: the human body is often described as 'made by human hands' because it has a human origin in human parents. When however the offertory prayer over the wine blesses God for 'this wine ... fruit of the vine and work of human hands' it seems to me to be going against the more usual ancient description of wine, which is to say wine is '*not* made by human hands'. Wine is more than human hands can create. Human beings can gather the grapes and press them, but the fermentation which changes grape-juice into wine is a gift of God, something beyond human powers. We have noticed already that wine stands for the divine life of Christ when placed beside the bread and the water which stands for his human body and his human life.

For example, St Justin, writing towards the end of the second century, is quite explicit: 'For as man did not make the blood of the vine, but God ...' (*Apologia* 32). Again Justin says: 'It was not man that engendered the blood of the grape, but God' (*Trypho* 76). We drink wine, and we even feel like gods: 'Wine, which cheers the heart of gods and men' (Judg 9:13). One of psalms speaks of God's making 'wine to gladden men's hearts' (Ps 103[104]:15).

When we drink from the chalice, the warmth of heart and the gladness which comes to us, even fleetingly, reminds us that we have received the divine life of Jesus. If we desire to thank God by doing works of imperishable love, then it is the divine power of Christ which will act in us, not our own weak selves. The old Christian prayer *Anima Christi* (Soul of Christ) has the line '*sanguis Christi, inebria me*', 'blood of Christ, intoxicate me'. There is a certain divine madness about many of the things a Christian finds himself doing for the love of God, and there is a sense in which he or she has to be intoxicated, drunk with the love of God, so that God is working, not the Christian. This divine power is often not felt when it is needed, but that does not mean the power is not there: it is there. But the experience of drinking the chalice is a preparation, a reassurance ahead of time, that Jesus will give us power to do his Father's will when the moments of trial come.

We could well join together in our minds the taking of the chalice and the more obviously divine days or moments of our lives. When we have a good day, a fine day in spring, a warm celebration, a magnificent concert, anything that uplifts our heart and makes us feel like kings or queens or someone divine, just for a day — then we can say to ourselves: 'This is what the chalice is promising me . . . but not yet'.

Of course, the body of Christ is divine also, and in any case Christ is not divided, and whoever receives his body receives his life too. We are dealing here only with the symbolism of bread, water and wine as it was understood in the early Church. The early Christians thought of the body of Christ as being from Mary, and therefore 'made by hands', but of his blood as being from God his Father, so 'not made by hands'. But when he shed his blood and the water from his body, his divinity was made clear and our humanity was redeemed; and in the resurrection his body too was 'spiritual' — that is, 'not made by hands' (cf. 1 Cor 15:44). The temple of his body was raised up again in three days, 'not made by human hands'. In the Eucharist we receive the risen Christ.

Prayer of the love of God

Father, my rock, my stronghold, listen to the prayer of one who wants to love you. If only I could see all the love you have given to me from the first moment of my existence until now, given to me as if I were your only child, then surely I would begin to love you back with real warmth and dedication. Have pity on my blindness. If only my heart could feel all the love you have given me over the years, then my answering love would be warm and constant and cheerful. What poor people we humans are, that we have to ask for the love to love with!

When the Spirit was sent by you and by your Son on the apostles and disciples at the first Pentecost, some of the crowd who heard and watched them thought they were drunk, full of new wine (cf. Acts 2:13). Fill me, fill all of us in your Church today, with the same new wine. Now that we may receive the chalice again at the Eucharist as in the early days of the Church, give us in huge measure that imperishable love which it signifies. Renew us through and through, so that the new wine does not come into old wine bottles, but into new (cf. Mk 2:22). As we eat the bread of life at your table, may it shout aloud to us of your love and protection, of your Spirit who hovers over us. May it speak in the words of your Son, telling us of your faithfulness and fatherliness. May your Spirit come down and make us all new, so that none of the wine of your love is lost, but that every drop will create joyful service in us, for all those in our lives whom we can help. Both the love, and the loving heart which alone can contain it, are of your creation, not man's. So, please . . .

'Blood of Christ, inebriate me', give me the courage of a drunken man, who can sometimes do things in that state which he would never dare sober. I know, my Lord Jesus, that any brave or praiseworthy things I have done in the past have been your doing more than mine. It only takes the cold morning truth of reality to bring out the coward in me, but when your grace and strength are with me, even most difficult tasks become easy. You already have my eyes, my ears, my tongue, my hands and feet, and my heart. When I drink the chalice of your blood, your life-blood, then surely you will come to life in me and begin to use all my bodily members as your own. My body should have become the 'new wine skin' or 'new bottle' for your new wine, because my body is no longer mine, but yours.

Is this, then, how you 'drink the fruit of the vine new, in the kingdom', as you said at your Last Supper: 'I shall not drink again of the fruit of the vine until that day when I drink it new in the kingdom of God'? (Mk 14:25). The kingdom of God is surely here already for you, though not yet for us in its fullness. And you are in me, this member of your body, drinking the wine which is your own life. And the manner of it is certainly a new thing.

So the intoxication, the drunkenness, I am asking for is your love taking over my life. Just now and then in my life the veil has been lifted from my eyes ever so little, and I have been, yes, like someone drunk, at the joy of your closeness, Jesus. But my feelings are of no great importance, so long as the reality is there, so long as you are really using my hands to do your work, and my heart to love with. May I love all your little ones, for the sake of God our Father, even if the world should hate me for doing so. Amen.

18

The precious blood of Christ

Until the publication of the new Roman Missal in 1970, there was in the Church's calendar a feast of The Precious Blood, which was not really thought of as a feast of the Eucharist. Since 1970, however, the feast has been united with the feast of the Body of Christ (*Corpus Christi*), which is now called The Body and Blood of Christ. The phrase 'precious blood' comes from the First Letter of Peter: 'You were ransomed . . . not with perishable things such as silver or gold, but with the precious blood of Christ, like that of a lamb without blemish or spot' (1 Pet 1:18f). We were 'ransomed', 'bought back', 'paid for', 'redeemed', according to the New Testament, and these words imply we were slaves or hostages until the blood of Christ won our freedom. The blood of Christ was 'precious', says St Peter, meaning that the redemption cost Jesus his life, it was a costly business. But the word 'precious' also means the opposite of 'perishable': 'precious' is another of the words used to describe things that come directly 'from God', 'not made by human hands'. No other blood than this would have been enough.

To whom was the ransom paid? St Paul tells us: 'You are not your own property, you have been bought and paid for' (1 Cor 6:20). The murder, and so the blood, of Jesus is on us all, but he has let us off the debt, freed us from responsibility for it, by forgiving us as we killed him. It is as though he put into our hands the price to pay our debt to him, a debt which would otherwise be completely beyond us. 'You were sacrificed, and with your blood you bought men for God of every race, language, people and nation and made them a line of kings and priests, to serve our God and to rule the world' (Rev 5:9f). The Church is 'the Church of God which he bought with his own blood' (Acts 20:28).

No one can buy the love of another. Most clearly, no one can pay for love 'with perishable things such as silver and gold' (1 Pet 1:18).

'Your silver perish with you, because you thought you could obtain the gift of God with money!' (Acts 8:20). The prophet Isaiah had foretold, 'Buy corn without money and eat, and, at no cost, wine and milk' (Is 55:1), so Jesus was very angry at the buyers and sellers and money changers in the temple, who made it seem as if the gift of God was up for sale. Even God cannot buy the love of human beings, for if he forced our wills we would no longer be human beings. Instead, after men had killed his only Son, through that Son he forgave us and ratified all the wonderful promises Jesus had made. Love can go no further than to say, 'Kill me and I shall still love you — *now* will you love me in return?'

In the language of sacrifice, to which the expression 'precious blood' first of all belongs, the sacrifice of Jesus on the cross was pleasing to God because his blood, being 'precious' or divine, far outshone in value any gift men could make — yet here was a man making the gift. This gift outshone others in value, because it was one with the prayer of God's only Son, and any parent listens to a cry like that. But Jesus in his prayer was insisting on taking all the rest of us with him: he the eldest brother, we the brothers and sisters. This was not his own idea, but his Father's, and Jesus willingly went to death for it. In the resurrection the Father through Jesus was able to make it clear to the witnesses that the promises were real. From then on we were able to know with certainty that in spite of our sins we are indeed divine sons and daughters of God.

'You have received without charge, give without charge' (Mt 10:8). We have received forgiveness without our having to pay for it; so we must forgive others who offend us even if they show no signs of being sorry.

Prayer of one redeemed

Jesus, my Redeemer, along with all the human race I was responsible for your death, just as today I am not able to say, 'Half the world is starving, but that has nothing to do with me!' What one of us does, all of us do, for we in exactly the same situation would do no better than the greatest sinner. In a real sense, your blood is on my hands. But you have turned our greatest sin into our greatest glory. Instead of being blamed for your blood as we deserve, we are invited to share your blood as blood-brothers and blood-sisters of yours, and first-generation sons and daughters of God. You have taken our debt away: no longer will we be cast into prison until we pay the last penny. How much is the price we owe for your blood? Is it thirty pieces of silver, the price Judas put on it, and then threw back at the authorities when he realized what he had done? (Mt 27:3). Is it ten thousand talents, the sum mentioned in one of your parables? (Mt 18:24). That comes to many millions of pounds of our money, but is no nearer the real price. Your precious blood is beyond price, beyond anything this heaven and earth holds. So how could we pay, how could we make a return? Instead you gave it to us as a gift; and if that sin is forgiven, then we know all lesser sins are forgiven, since we know now the height and the depth and the width of your Father's mercy, which is truly infinite. No gaoler, no prison authority, no judge, no executioner, no angel, no devil can imprison us now, for your precious blood is the key which opens, and no one can close (cf. Rev 37). All the more urgently, then, I ask you to bless my enemies, and to make me gentle and forgiving with all who offend me. For unless I live in your world, the 'new heaven and new earth' where forgiveness reigns, then I will be back in prison, guilty of your blood by my own choice.

Father of Jesus, who are my Father also, the riches you have placed in my hands do indeed intoxicate me. To be able to walk out of prison a free man, to know that you who have saved me desire that I stay free, to know that the sun and the moon and the stars are all mine again, and the endless beauty of the world, from the tiniest flower to the greatest mountain. And all men and women are my friends, my sisters and brothers. I can speak to them now knowing they are as close to you as I am. Even in those who seem hostile, there is underneath their roughness the heart of a child to which I can speak. Let me never despise the least of your little ones, for that would be to risk shedding the precious blood all over again. Your Son Jesus has brought every last one of them to be his own sister or brother, so let me never stand between him and them.

Take away all greed and love of money from our hearts, dear Father. Let your bread, and your Son's incorruptible love be all my desire. Once we have seen the beauty of your gift, how endlessly precious it is, may we never hanker for shameful gain (1 Pet 5:2).

Let your Church authorities never be tainted with greed for earthly money (cf. Mk 12:38ff) after living so close to the body and blood of Christ Jesus. Make us willing to give up all our perishable wealth to secure your heavenly gift, when the day of our death comes, or sooner should you call us so, to witness to your true values (cf. Mk 10:21). Do not let the thorns and thistles of greed choke the growth of true love in our hearts (cf. Mk 4:19). I am afraid of them, because weeds so often disguise themselves to look like fruitful plants. Let me never be entrapped or imprisoned again. Deliver us all from evil. Amen.

19

Precious metal

Simon, son of John, was given by Jesus the new name Cephas or Peter, meaning 'rock' (Jn 1:42). From then on Peter seems to have been specially alert to metaphors about rocks, stones and precious metals. As the apostle John liked to describe the Church of Jesus' disciples in the image of a vine and its branches, and Paul's favourite image for the same reality was that of a body and its head, so for Peter the dominant image is of a temple of living stones, with Christ the chosen and precious cornerstone (1 Pet 24:4ff). We find indications of Peter's way of thinking mainly in Mark's gospel (Mark having been a disciple of Peter's), in Peter's speeches in the *Acts of the Apostles*, and in the *First Letter of Peter*.

We shall return later to the idea of 'precious stones', but we could here consider the allied image of precious metals, gold and silver which come from rock and are refined by fire out of the rock in which they are embedded. Peter's first letter says, 'This is a cause of great joy for you, even though you may for a short time have to bear being plagued by all sorts of trials; so that, when Jesus Christ is revealed, your faith will have been tested and proved like gold — only it is more precious than gold, which is corruptible even though it bears testing by fire — and then you will have praise and glory and honour' (1 Pet 1:6f). Gold is perishable, but the process of making imperishable faith is similar to the refining process. The whole must be tested by fire, so that the precious element can be separated off. 'You were redeemed ... not with perishable things such as silver and gold, but with the precious blood of Christ' (1 Pet 1:18f). 'Not ... decoration of gold, and wearing of robes, but ... the imperishable jewel of a gentle and quiet spirit, which in God's sight is very precious' (1 Pet 3:3f).' I have no silver or gold, but I give you what I have' (Acts 3:4). 'Your silver perish with you!' (Acts 8:20).

If we follow the story of Peter in the second half of Mark's gospel, he starts out already having some faith he has just confessed that Jesus is the Christ, at the end of the first half of the gospel (Mk 8:29). But then Jesus begins to talk about his coming violent death, and this Peter cannot stomach (Mk 8:32). Jesus then says, 'Whoever is ashamed of me and of my words . . . of him will the Son of Man also be ashamed' (Mk 8:38). Then comes the transfiguration, when the Father's voice from heaven says of Jesus, 'This is my beloved Son; listen to him' (Mk 9:7). In the next recorded incident, the disciples were unable to cast out a dumb and deaf spirit from a young epileptic boy, because they had not prayed. The boy's father had faith, but not yet a strong enough faith (Mk 9:14–29). Peter would not pray or could not pray in the Garden of Gethsemane, in spite of Jesus' frequent warnings to 'watch and pray' (e.g., Mk 13:35). He had faith, but not enough: he had not prayed for a stronger faith. Shortly afterwards, he was found asleep, and then he denied the Son of Man before men, when he was on trial at the fire in the courtyard of the high priest (cf. Mk 14:66ff). Peter was as good as deaf to what the voice from heaven had said, and he was certainly dumb when it came to speaking up for Jesus and admitting that he was indeed a disciple of Jesus. At the fire . . . would the gospel writers have remembered what Peter was doing at the time, standing at the fire and warming himself, if Peter himself had not later seen this incident as the time when his own faith was burnt away from the dross, to become imperishable love?

Jesus, on the other hand, did pray in the Garden before his trial. And on trial he did answer up — or the Spirit within him answered (Mk 13:11) — echoing the words spoken at his transfiguration. He said, 'I am the Christ, the Son of the Blessed' (Mk 14:61f). The blood in his veins, blood of the Son of God, was proof against the fire of persecution. He went on to shed his blood rather than deny who he was. But Peter 'the doorkeeper' was asleep when the master of the house came at cock crow (Mk 13:35f). The foundation in Peter was sound, but what Peter had recently built on the foundation was still too full of himself, and therefore perishable (1 Cor 3:9–17).

Prayer of one facing persecution

Jesus, my most precious Lord, be ever near me as this time of trial approaches. Perhaps one day like an old campaigner I shall look

F

back on this time of preparation as something glorious; but here and now I feel anything but glorious. Yet my task is simple: to speak out what in any case the blood in my veins cries out, that I am a child of God and that you are my own brother. From that it will be obvious to anyone with eyes to see, that if you accept me as a brother, you must be willing to accept any man, woman or child as your brother or sister for what have I to recommend to you except my great need?

Help me to learn from the story of your apostle and friend St Peter as it is told in St Mark's gospel. Open my ears to hear what your Father said to you at your transfiguration, and to hear what you were saying to Peter. Grant that I may not fall asleep while you pray before your chalice, but that I may be wide awake and praying: 'I believe; help my unbelief!' (Mk 9:24). If anything within me tells me to be quiet, let me pray all the more insistently, 'Jesus, Son of David, have mercy on me!' (Mk 10:48), and again, 'Help my unbelief!' Turn my untried faith into pure and powerful love. Peter's case is consoling, because his faith was purified and became precious, imperishable love through the shame of his failure in the high priest's courtyard. Like Peter, I am so inclined to trust my own strength and blunder into temptation, following you into places where I am not yet ready to go. Like him, like the epileptic boy, I throw myself into the fire and into the water, where in turn I am burnt and I sink like a stone (Mk 9:22).

Open my ears to hear, and open my mouth to tell the world that you have chosen me for your son — just as indeed you have chosen all those who are ill-disposed towards me, did they but know it. You are telling them to listen to me, so I must speak up: 'Yes, I am a disciple of Jesus; yes, I am one of them; no, I am not a Galilean, but I do know the man you are speaking of. Yes, I am another Christ; I have been adopted as a son of the Blessed'. Let your blood cry out from my veins. The day of my Confirmation was the day of my transfiguration, if I only had eyes to see. Transfigure me again when I receive your chalice at the Eucharist, so that I may remember the warmth of the fire of your Spirit as I come closer to the time of trial, for then my heart will be cold.

I pray that I may not have to go through the ordeal of shame and failure as Peter had to. But if that is to be my way as well, bring me through even that ordeal as you brought him through his, to an invincible strength beyond.

Abba, Father, if it be possible let this chalice pass from me. Nevertheless, not what I want but what you want. Many people would find the trial that I am facing rather trivial, but to me here and now it is not trivial. Give me please the simplicity of a child, *your* child. When people try to confuse me and trip me up, make me remember that the one and only thing that matters to me under the sun is your fatherly love for me. All the sorrow and shame we pass through is only so much refining fire, removing from us our love for anything less than you. Sooner or later all that is not you will have to go: then let it be sooner rather than later. My Father, fill me with your Spirit, who will speak up for me in my hour of trial as you promised through your Son Jesus. Transfigure me; transform me into his likeness so that his precious blood in me may triumph over all human trials.

20
Good Shepherd

One of the hopes of the people in the time of Jesus was that God would keep his promise about the Shepherd. The prophet Ezekiel has a chapter all about Yahweh (God) as the Shepherd (Ezek 34). The shepherds of Israel were feeding themselves instead of feeding the sheep; their whole attitude towards the sheep was to exploit them as much as possible. So God said there would be a day of reckoning: 'I am going to look after my flock myself, and keep all of it in view'. He would gather it together again from all the places where it had been scattered, take it out of the control of the shepherds, and himself 'look for the lost one, bring back the stray, bandage the wounded and make the weak strong'; he would watch over the fat and healthy, and be a true Shepherd to them. Either by himself or through his servant David, the shepherd-king, he would make them lie down in good pasture by running streams, and feed them so that they would never be short of food. One of the psalms, 'The Lord is my shepherd', adds the detail that the pasture will be in meadows of green grass (Ps 22[23]:2).

In the gospel stories we find many hints that in Jesus is the fulfilment of these prophecies. For instance, in the sixth chapter of Mark's gospel, Jesus makes his last visit to a synagogue, in his home town. Already he could no longer openly enter any other town of Galilee. But if he cannot enter the synagogues the people, the sheep, can come out to him; and they do come out in their thousands. There Jesus has pity on them, because they are like sheep without a shepherd. Away from the influence of the synagogue rulers, and beyond the reach of King Herod the false shepherd-king, Jesus teaches the crowds at length, feeding their minds. Then with the help of his apostles and other disciples he makes all the people lie down on the green grass beside the waters of the lake, and he feeds them himself with the loaves and the fish until they are satisfied. Plenty of food is left over.

As the time of his passion drew nearer, Jesus began to make clear to his followers that the Shepherd of Yahweh would have to die, even though he was the King, the Son of David. At the Last Supper he reminded the apostles of the passage in scripture, 'I will strike the shepherd and the sheep will be scattered' (Zech 13:7), a prophecy they were unwilling to understand. In the beautiful chapter of John's gospel about the Good Shepherd, Jesus says, 'The good shepherd is one who lays down his life for his sheep' (Jn 10). Thus we have, even in the image of the Shepherd, a place for the bread, and the water, and the wine of the Eucharist. Jesus fed the crowd of five thousand and more with bread. Beside them were the waters, flowing as they do from the mountains north of the Sea of Galilee along the Jordan southwards to the Dead Sea. The Shepherd feeds the sheep and finds them water to drink. But then he invites those who can hear the call, to come and be shepherds with him, to take the chalice which will mean their death (one way or another), to be ready to lay down their lives for the sheep as he would himself. After his resurrection and ascension, the people would then follow the disciples and Peter as they led the way to the gathering of the sheep in Christ: 'He is going before you to Galilee; it is there you will see him, just as he told you' (Mk 16:7). The Shepherd goes in front: while there is still some distance to go we do not see him face to face.

Not all the sheep are transformed to become shepherds. Yet Jesus died for the poor hungry crowds just as surely as he died for those who would become shepherds. The only people unimpressed were the false shepherds, the 'wolves' (Mt 10:16) from whom the people were being rescued. Their rich incomes and the honour in which they were held were at stake (Mk 12:38ff). They made sure that the destiny of the shepherd included a cup of suffering.

Prayer of a lamb of God

My Father, great Shepherd, I thank you for revealing yourself to us in such a loving and lovable image. I thank you that before the stars were created you chose me to be one of your lambs, one of your yearlings, one of your sheep. When you promised through your prophet Ezekiel to come yourself and gather your scattered flock together, even he did not know how much he was saying. He was thinking, surely, of the scattered people of Judah in exile in Babylon and Egypt and various other places far from the ruins of Jerusalem, and of how you would none the less recreate the nation back in the land of Judah. But now we know that in Jesus your Son and (under you) our good shepherd, you meant to gather all your scattered children, of every race, nation and tongue, into your one flock. I and my family never belonged to your original flock of Israel, but though we came from another sheepfold your Son has died to save us from the wolves, and has become for us the door into your sheepfold.

Your care is with us always. If we are lost, you will find us; if we stray, you will bring us back. If we are wounded, you will bandage us; if we are weak you will make us strong; if we are fat and healthy you will watch over us: you will be a true shepherd to us. In our daily or weekly Eucharist you first of all feed our minds and hearts through your word in the scriptures, then you give us our food under the sign of bread, the body of Christ your Son. The living water brought to us by Jesus wells up in our hearts, telling us always that we are your children, and the sheep of your flock. Open my eyes to see how you have cared for me as if I were the apple of your eye, all these years — both in the favours you have shown me and in the wonderful work of your Son on my behalf. Open my ears to hear your voice calling my name. Open my lips to tell you that I am yours.

Prayer of one called to be a shepherd

Jesus, Good Shepherd and my King, in your own day you called only a few to become apostles and disciples, compared with the huge numbers in the crowds that followed you. But now you call all those who are confirmed in your Church to become shepherds. By our Baptism we are sheep and lambs in God's flock; by our Confirmation we are called to be shepherds. As children we are cared for by others in your name; but as we grow up we are asked to take on responsibility for others, either as parents or teachers or pastors or nurses, or in whatever way serving the needs of a few or of the general public. Even children at school or older children in a family are learning to take over as shepherds one day. We learn, from the quality of the love that was shown to us, how to love others and care for them. As lambs and sheep we followed you; when we are called to be shepherds we cease to be simply sheep following a shepherd and we become one with you the shepherd. Your power works through us, if we are good shepherds, and we have nothing to boast about. You will not judge us by how well we succeeded as shepherds: when all is said and done, we do not ourselves know the way to the green pastures. We have to follow you the chief shepherd (1 Pet 5:4), and we are in reality more like sheepdogs, who are useless unless they constantly hear and see the signals of their chief shepherd.

When we think of the small number of Christians in the world, and of our very mixed quality, we are indeed still only a few disciples compared with the huge number for whom you died, and we are not very successful. Please as we take the chalice give us the strength and inspiration to spend our lives for the flock, or for the small section of it that you have entrusted to us. Keep us from ever turning into wolves ourselves, preying on the flock; give us your power and goodness to stand up to the wolves there already are. In the hour of our death, come looking for each one of us, for in that hour each of us will be only a lamb of God.

21

The Servant

Jesus was not only the Good Shepherd, and the King of David's line, and the Son of Man who will come on the clouds of heaven; he was also the Servant of Yahweh. There are four songs about the Servant in the second part of the book of the prophet Isaiah. In our liturgy we read them as the first readings of Monday, Tuesday, Wednesday and Good Friday in Holy Week. This was the aspect of Jesus' teaching that Peter found most difficult to take, because the Servant in the prophecy is one who goes through increasingly severe sufferings and even dies, before coming into glory. Peter and the other apostles found the thought of glory agreeable, but when Jesus began to say plainly he must be killed first, they were very perplexed and confused. Yet there was no doubt about Jesus' teaching. In the first half of Mark's gospel there was hardly any hint of sufferings to come, but as soon as Peter has said to Jesus, 'You are the Christ' (Mk 8:29), Jesus begins to speak openly about his coming death, and from then on, all the rest of the gospel is about the passion, with many indications that the gospel writer knows Jesus went to death with his eyes open and willingly. The ideas of 'servant' and 'death for others' are closely linked, as when Jesus says, 'For the Son of Man also came not to be served but to serve, and to give his life as a ransom for many' (Mk 10:45). The first half of Mark's gospel has Jesus making journeys which double back and forth and around, but once Jesus begins to speak openly of his death (Mk 8:31), he makes a straight unswerving journey to Jerusalem.

After the resurrection, it was these 'Servant Songs' which Jesus brought back to the minds of the apostles and disciples, in asking them, 'Was it not ordained that the Christ should suffer and so enter into his glory?' (Lk 24:26). Or rather, these songs were among the passages of scripture he opened their minds and hearts to understand, since the gospel writers and other New Testament authors make quite clear that they now understand Jesus to have been the Suffering Servant of Yahweh. In the very early days of the Church, it seems to have been common in prayer to God to refer to Jesus as 'your holy servant Jesus' (Acts 4:27).

The *First Letter of Peter* has a theme about the Servant running all through it: Jesus the Servant suffered although he was righteous; so we servants will suffer also, but let it be for being righteous, not because we deserve to be punished. St Paul also often comes back to the theme: 'And if we are children we are heirs as well: heirs of God and coheirs with Christ, sharing his sufferings so as to share his glory' (Rom 8:17). Jesus, 'though his state was divine, emptied himself, taking the form of a servant' (Phil 2:6).

Why does a servant of God have to drink the cup of suffering? Partly because those who are slaves of evil cannot understand the good intentions of God's servant. They misunderstand him, and want to get rid of him because of what they think his intentions are. In doing God's will, he inevitably comes up against the dead weight of sinful mankind, and it breaks his heart. But if he dies willingly, still wanting to help those who have let him down, then there is a hope of heaven for his enemies. If those who are grasping and the one they have robbed can share this world, because the one robbed never complained, there is a chance they can share eternity as well.

Jesus did not only speak of service in terms of dying for people, but also in the ordinary ways of service: we remember how he washed the feet of the Twelve before the Last Supper (Jn 13), and told them to do the same. In this as in all things he was imitating his Father, whom he knew so much better than we do. From the beginning of time, the Father has been at the service of mankind. We talk about Providence, but at the same time what is meant is that the Father has served us without ceasing, with so little return of love from us.

Prayer of one who is sick

Mary, lowly handmaid of God, you served him so well, now he must surely do anything you wish. Come with me to Jesus, and then with Jesus and me to the Father, to ask for this grace: to see some point, some purpose, in my sickness even while I suffer. I like to think, if there were people attacking me I could feel one with Jesus and forgive them. But when my enemy is an illness, how do I forgive that, what is the use of that?

Your Son Jesus invites me to take his chalice and drink from it. I pray that his wine in me, his divine life in me, may go to the very depths of my body and mind and heart, to transform me into a new creature beyond the reach of sickness. In the meantime, stupid though it seems, I forgive the disease which attacks me, and I believe stubbornly that my sufferings too are useful for many, as Jesus' sufferings were useful for all. Let me too be a servant of God our Father; let me not blame him for my sickness, but let me take it as one of the burdens of this sinful world he is asking me to help him carry, not for ever but for a time, on the way to glory. Ask these things for me, of your Son and of our Father. And thank you, my Mother, for your constant love and service to me.

Jesus, Suffering Servant, see how I come with your mother to ask you to take me and my sufferings and make my destiny one with yours. Let the cup that you drank and the cup that I drink be one and the same. Where you in your sufferings had to hold yourself back from hating your enemies or from despairing of God's help, so let me in my sufferings be gentle and patient, not lashing out, because of the pain inside me, at those who try to help me, not ceasing to believe in our Father's tender love. Jesus, let me go side by side with you, and be a part of the solution to this world's sorrows, and not just a burden upon others. Even in this life, those of us who die of an illness not yet curable are of service to some coming generation, because the doctors will come by experience and our sufferings to understand the causes and the cure. But the greatest service must surely be, as yours was, to go on believing in our Father's love although we ourselves are dying in pain. The centurion at the foot of the cross had seen those mocking you; then he saw how you died. And in his own way he believed in you rather than in them. May my life and death make others say, 'Truly, here was a son of God' (Mk 15:39).

Loving Father, I come with Jesus and with Mary to ask you to take me in my sufferings as your servant. Help me to see beyond the pains of my present life to the glory ahead, and widen my heart so that I can take with me all those in my world whom Jesus has served and saved. If it be that I get better from my illness, let me go to any lengths to teach others about your love. But in sickness or in health, I say to you with the Prodigal Son, 'Father, I am not worthy to be called your son: let me be like one of your paid servants' (Lk 15:21). Then again I am afraid that my service will be so poor, that in the end I will have to say, 'Father, I am not worthy to be called your servant let me be simply your child'. The 'children of this world' put so much effort into the causes they follow, they would put me to shame.

Thank you, Father, for the countless years of service you have given to me, in preparing a world for me and for all those I love. Thank you too for all you have prepared for us in your kingdom, the glory you have promised us when our short time of suffering and service is over. You have prepared it for us through your holy servant Jesus.

22

My Father's will

A good servant is always alert to do the will of his master. Although Jesus was divine, he emptied himself to become a servant. All his life he was seeking to do his Father's will. It was as if Jesus had taken on the fallen nature of us prodigal sons and daughters, and was saying, 'Father, although I have not sinned against you, my brothers and sisters have sinned. We are no longer worthy to be called your children: let us be like your paid servants'. In one breath he is calling us his sisters and brothers but promising on our behalf that we will behave like good servants if he shows us the way. Once we know how endlessly forgiving our Father is, then we shall be able to give our whole heart and soul to his service, because we no longer need have any fear of failure.

We are not servants, we are children, so we only work our short lifetime *as if* we were servants. Jesus for his part worked throughout his short lifetime as if he were sinner alongside us sinners. As we have seen, he was, to speak again in symbols, divine wine mixed with our bread-and-water humanity. His body and human spirit was from Mary, his divine life from God. When he shed his blood he was one of us, but shedding divine blood. The love he showed in dying was beyond human power. From that moment it was as if his blood given him by his Father transformed his body and his human life, for when he was seen again his body too was a spiritual, imperishable body, and he was beyond the reach of human death. Somewhere in that mystery we become in truth God's children, our blood becomes divine, and the same resurrection is promised to us. The truth still holds: what one of us does, all of us share in. On the day of our death the divine blood in us will transform us also, by the power of our Father.

Jesus sometimes called his Father's will his 'cup' or chalice: 'Am I not to drink the cup my Father has given me?' (Jn 18:11). He also meant by it what we would call our conscience. My conscience, what I judge I ought to do here and now, is the same as my cup, and my Father's will. In our sacrament of Confirmation, we celebrate the wonderful fact that God is always calling us. In receiving the chalice at Mass, we celebrate the same truth as it applies today. Today I know, or I seek to know, what is my Father's will. I take the cup and I am saying, 'Not my will, but yours. Let what you have said be done to me', and I am asking for the divine power to do what should be done.

Conscience, like the cup, is also something to be shared. Many of my decisions I must make on my own, but many others are a matter for a group to decide: in a family, in a business, as a local community, as a national community, in various interest groups to which we belong. If we are all Christians in a group, then the sharing in the chalice is a sharing in God's will. Often, it will be possible for Christian or Catholic groups to share with one another the difficult choices and decisions each one is faced with in his or her own life; then a sharing in the chalice will bring an added strength for each to take back to his or her separate non-Christian groups at work or in the community.

Jesus is our model of obedience. For him, to seek God's will was to find it; to find it was to do it. Jesus must have been deeply conscious that everything the Father had planned and done for him and for his people in the past had come from heaven with complete goodwill. There was nothing to be feared in following the Father's will, because the goodwill would continue the same as ever. The rest of us often have doubts: have we really found God's wills? Is his will going to bring us happiness? Can we bear the pains and disappointments that lie between us and happiness? We should really be no more uneasy taking the chalice and drinking from it, than we are in taking the body of Christ, the food of the children, where we know there is only peace and comfort of heart.

Prayer of union with God

Father, your Son has told us, 'You must call no one on earth your father, since you have only one Father, and he is in heaven' (Mt 23:9). Whatever authority over us any human person may have, if your will is different from theirs, then we must follow your will, not theirs. In the last resort, we must decide for ourselves what is right (cf. Lk 12:57), since in our conscience we are alone with you. To go forward to do what you want is the same as to take the cup and drink from it: your will for us is good, and you will provide the power to fulfil it.

What a joy it is, this two-way traffic, this constant conversation, between you and me. Each morning I recall your unfailing kindness; all through the day you present me with your will to follow; when I fail you forgive me; when all goes well I can see that it was your strength and your inspiration that carried me through; and then I have even more to thank you for.

Jesus was always your Son, but who he was became clearest in his trial and death. As when a composer writes a symphony, the symphony is not fully revealed until the last chord dies away. Father, let my life be such that those who see me and deal with me may find you. For this I need to be always seeking your will as Jesus did — either that or truly sorry when I have strayed from your will to please myself.

We human beings get so attached to selfish pleasures, or money and the things it can buy; or else we get tired of high ideals and settle for something more comfortable; or we go for places and situations where we know we will be highly thought of. Help us, Father, when we have the opportunity, to stand back and come to ourselves and be with you alone; and there with the grace of your Son and the Spirit, to let you detach us from all the things we put in your place, so that you alone may be all in all to us.

Father, we need zeal too, to find out what your will may be in difficult choices: from the scriptures, from the teachings of the popes and the bishops and other wise men, both inside and outside the Church, from our friends and advisers and our fellow Christians, and above all from prayer. We know that if we decide wrongly even after prayer and discussion and study, you will bring us back into the truth as you brought Abraham to realize the truth. If we have goodwill, you can and will teach us the rest.

The people in Jerusalem chose a rebel, Barabbas. Father, make me and all your servants trusting and obedient. Take our vineyard and make it fruitful for you. And when choosing your will seems like madness, because of what might happen to us, bring to our minds the love and trust your Son Jesus showed you. Only three days after his terrible death, his mother and the disciples already knew how right he was to trust you.

23

Lamb of God

When Jesus first said, 'This is my body' and 'This is my blood' he also said, 'Do this in memory of me'. So we are told in Luke's gospel (Lk 22:19) and by St Paul (1 Cor 11:24f) and in the words of the Mass. The stress is on the word '*me*': 'Do not do this any more in memory of Moses: do it in memory of me'. There seems to be some doubt among scripture scholars as to whether the Last Supper was the passover meal, or whether perhaps the passover feast itself was on the next day, Friday (Jn 18:28). But there can be no doubt that the books of the New Testament are telling us that the Last Supper and the suffering and death of Jesus are a new passover, are in fact the real passover, of which the ancient Jewish story and its rite were only a shadow, a foretaste and a promise. The real passover is from slavery to sin into the freedom of the children of God; the real paschal lamb is Jesus, sacrificed so we could be saved; the promised prophet like Moses (Deut 18:18; Acts 3:22) is Jesus, leading his people to safety and a new life through the waters of Baptism.

The story of the first passover is told in the book of *Exodus*. The Hebrew people made ready to escape from Egypt and slavery under the pretext of going out into the wilderness to offer sacrifice. Their last meal was the passover meal: each household took a year-old unblemished male lamb or kid, killed it, prepared and roasted it, and then ate standing up. Some of the blood of the animal was sprinkled on the doorposts and the lintel of the house, then the plague would pass over the Hebrew houses and only strike the first-born of the Egyptians. Later, the Hebrews would have to redeem or buy back all their first-born sons and first-born animals, because God had spared their first-born on this night (Ex 12 and 13). There were obviously many families or households of the Hebrew people involved in the escape, so there were many paschal lambs or kids. But Jesus is the passover lamb for just one household or family; he is food enough for all his family and his blood brings God's protection to all. The hymn sung to the Lamb in the vision of John says, 'You were sacrificed, and with your blood you bought men for God, of every race, language, people and nation, and made them a line of kings and priests to serve our God and to rule the world' (Rev 4:9f).

Jesus is also like Moses, the one who rallies his people and readies them to escape to freedom through the waters. When the enemy chariots were seen coming in pursuit, Moses cried, 'Have no fear! Stand firm, and you will see what Yahweh will do to save you today: the Egyptians you see today, you will never see again. Yahweh will do the fighting for you; you have only to keep still' (Ex 14:13f). Our enemy today is the weakness within us which tells us we will be abandoned by God because we have not done enough for him, or because we have done wrong. Jesus tells us to have no fear: he is taking us to the other shore where we are children of God, every one a 'first-born son' (Heb 12:23), the daughters just as important as the sons (cf. Gal 3:28), all first-born children. Our Father accepts our efforts no matter how humble, and forgives our enormous short-comings. The enemy cannot touch us any more.

In a way which seems strange to us, wine may have been used for washing in early times: Jacob in blessing his son Judah says, 'He washes his coat in wine, his cloak in the blood of the grape' (Gen 49:11). From this comes the picture in *Revelation* of the people in heaven who had been through the great persecution: 'They have washed their robes white again in the blood of the Lamb' (Rev 7:14). White robes are almost the uniform of heaven-dwellers in scripture, and we still use white garments for those who are baptized.

Prayer of a first-born

THE FIRST-BORN SPEAKS: *Jesus, passover lamb*, Lord of Lords and King of Kings (Rev 17:14), again we can only thank you. You are the first-born, the only-begotten Son of God, but you gave up your position to share it with each of us, from the greatest to the least. This was not simply a question of going from the highest place in the banquet to take the lower place: you became one of us and you gave your very life, your human life, as a sacrifice to make sure we would all escape from the clutches of pride and fear. Then you led us to

83

take *your* rightful place in heaven, each of us loved by your Father as if he had no other child. Bitter herbs for you, and for us unleavened bread and the spotless lamb whose blood defended the doorway (Ex 12:7f). Thank you for telling us to do these things in memory of you, as we do at our Eucharist.

I have already prayed to you to make me a new person, with a new heart of flesh filled with your blood, filled with your life. Give to me now, if it please you, and to all of us the white garments of those who dwell in heaven, of those who 'have washed their robes white again in the blood of the Lamb'. Let us be children of the resurrection, like the young men in dazzling white garments who were seen at your resurrection. Surely the whiteness of my baptismal robe is no longer without stain or blemish as it was on the day of my Baptism?

THE LAMB REPLIES: Your robe is still as white as on the day you were baptized. Your robe is nothing but my Father's favour resting on you. What your family were celebrating on that day was the fact that my Father chose you, chose to call you his son; and he loves you as much today as ever he did. Nothing you can do will ever alter his affection for you. In his eyes you are a delight, because you are his. If he is not complaining about stains and blemishes, then they do not exist, because he is the truth. Your beauty is in the eye of your Father as he beholds you.

THE FIRST-BORN SPEAKS: Then your blood marked us out already as your Father's children, and this was why no plague could overtake us. Is there no difference, then, between your glory as you were baptized in the Jordan, and the dazzling white of your garments at your transfiguration, when they were whiter than any earthly fuller could bleach them?

JESUS, LAMB OF GOD, REPLIES: What God has shown to you through me, he can show to others through you. In the history of our family there have been many lambs sacrificed, many innocent victims of injustice and greed, who died and gave their lives, sometimes shedding their blood as I did, to help save their brothers and sisters. Every follower of mine is first of all given the gift of God: you were all redeemed by my blood. But then you are invited to do as I did, and lay down your life for others, whether by a life of hard work, or a life of suffering, or even by martyrdom. If you are truly mine, then the love of God becomes visible in you to those who are seeking. If you are a sickly or weak child, my glory goes to you and perhaps no further: fear not, it will be enough for you. If you are strong (remember, the *weak* are the strong), you become a lamb of God for others, a mirror in which they can see the glory of my love, as I was for you a mirror of the glory of my Father's love.

THE FIRST-BORN: Clothe me then in these glorious garments, if first you make me strong enough to wear them, and wise enough to remember always that the glory is yours. But above all, let me and all your great family be where we will never hunger or thirst again; where neither the sun nor scorching wind will ever plague us, because you, the Lamb who are at the throne, will be our orchard and will lead us to springs of living water, and God will wipe away all tears from our eyes (Rev 7:16f).

24
From earth, from heaven

The scriptures have a way of talking about what comes from earth and what comes from heaven, using many different phrases to mean the same two things. What comes from the earth is perishable, worthless, made by human hands; what comes from heaven is imperishable, precious, not made by human hands. From the earth comes weakness; from heaven comes power. Earthly things belong to this present age; heavenly things belong to the age to come, even if they are occasionally seen (and always present) here and now. The first covenant with Moses belonged to the present age; the new covenant sealed by Jesus belongs to the age to come. 'The first man (Adam), being from the earth, is earthly by nature, the second man (Christ) is from heaven' (1 Cor 15:47).

Some experiences in the life of man are shown to him as being unmistakably from God. He knows that God has spoken to him; he knows God has shown him what he sees. Such were the experiences of the chosen women and the apostles and the other witnesses of the resurrection. From then on they had to obey God and preach the risen Christ, no matter how many merely human authorities told them to be quiet (cf. Acts 4:19f). When Mark's gospel describes the transfiguration of Jesus, he says the clothes of Jesus 'became dazzlingly white, whiter than any earthly bleacher could make them' (Mk 9:3). Therefore the glory of them came from heaven.

The early Christian writer St Ignatius of Antioch has one sentence which contains several of these contrasts between 'earthly' and 'heavenly', showing how both aspects are there in one and the same person (*To the Ephesians* 7:2):

'There is one physician
both fleshly   and spiritual
born   and unborn
being in the flesh   God

in death	true life
both from Mary	and from God
first able to suffer	and then beyond suffering
Jesus Christ	our Lord'.

Jesus in the Garden of Gethsemane was feeling his weakness, and must have been tempted to run away. But he prayed for power; he prayed to his Father with whom all things are possible, who has power enough to conquer all things. Being weak, he prayed for power; being in flesh, he prayed in the Spirit, to God as his *Abba*, his own Father (cf. Gal 4:6). Even Jesus had to pray. As he said to Peter there in the garden, 'The spirit is willing, but the flesh is weak' (Mk 14:38), and Jesus shared our flesh. The (bread-and-water) humanity of Jesus was weak; only his spiritual, divine nature (his blood) was imperishable. When his weak human body shed his blood in a way that was seen to be unmistakably from God — so divinely loving was it — then our weak human nature was re-created. The way was open. The bridge, or the ladder, was built. What one of us does, all of us can do.

The experiences of the witnesses to the resurrection of Jesus convinced them once and for all that God is as Jesus revealed him. So God is our *Abba* also, and this faith makes all the actions of a Christian quite different from what they were before. There is something of heaven in them. From that day on we have as a sure foundation God's love for each of us as if we were his only child, and this whether we succeed or fail in doing his will. But if we want our faith to grow into divine love for others, we like Jesus will have to pray. 'You should be awake, and praying' (Mk 14:38).

Prayer of one who desires to ascend to God

Father, most high God, since before the fabled tower of Babel (Gen 11) the people of earth have been trying to reach up to you in heaven. Like the builders of the tower, they have used materials made by human hands, mortal lives and mortal thoughts, and their efforts were doomed to failure. Much truer was the vision of Jacob (Gen 28) who saw a ladder let down from heaven. Jesus your own Son was to claim that the vision of Jacob was fulfilled in him, the

Son of Man (Jn 1:51). If ever anyone enters your presence, it must be at your invitation, for no one knows the way except your Son and those to whom he reveals you.

We do not believe that all human life is worthless, but it is worthless in this respect, that it is totally unable to reach you by trying. We must wait to be picked up, like so many little children. When your Son Jesus promised us his body and blood as our Eucharist, he did not say that only his blood was divine: he said also, 'This is the bread that comes down from heaven' (Jn 6:50), meaning his body. Jesus as we receive him in the Eucharist is our risen Lord, so his body is the temple rebuilt in three days, rebuilt surely not by human hands (Jn 2:19). Yet his body was the same body, was it not, Father? All his mortal life was precious, was it not, and taken up for ever to heaven? And can you not make immortal all the good things of our own lives as well? I believe you can (cf. 2 Cor 5:4). Our body and human spirit is perishable, but you can make it imperishable through the precious blood of Jesus.

Father, has not mankind always been 'spirit, soul and body'? Have we not always been, by your gift, wine, water and bread? But the 'wine' in us was still but a 'grape'. Your Spirit was always at work in man, preparing us for the coming of your Son, as today your Spirit is at work in all who do not know your Son, so many human beings whom you certainy have not deserted. All men, women and children everywhere have always been your children, but so many of them have no idea that they are your children, or what a difference this could make to their lives. Your Son taught us who you are, where we come from, what you are like, and how to pray to you. He taught us to clink to him, the ladder, so that we may be lifted into heaven.

Truly good people are those who trust so well in your mercy that they are not afraid of falling. They take risks. On the foundation of faith laid by your Son, they build a world of goodness knowing that they themselves are nothing, for the power is yours. They climb up the ladder of Jacob. But I need not be jealous of them, I who never seem to get very far up the ladder, for even if they reach you first, none of them can take my place in your heart. And I remember the man we call the Good Thief: by your power he did more good in the hour before he died than most of us will ever do in a lifetime. He said one sentence: 'Lord, remember me when you come into your kingdom'; to which Jesus replied with the promise, 'Today you will be with me in paradise' (cf. Lk 23:39–43). All down the ages weak sinners have been encouraged by that conversation, started by a sinner.

My Father, 'the spirit is willing but the flesh is weak'. May I never lose hold of Jesus, your Son and my saviour. He stood on the earth and called up to you, 'Abba, Father!' You raised him to your side, and now he is my ladder to you. May the blood within me make me live as he lived, speak as he spoke, think as he thought, love as he loved.

25

The inner sanctuary

The *Letter to the Hebrews* in the ninth chapter makes a comparison between the body of Christ and the outer sanctuary of the temple (the Holy Place), and then between the blood of Christ and the inner sanctuary (the Holy of Holies). The whole sanctuary was like one tent, divided into the two compartments. In the outer was the lampstand, the table and the presentation loaves. In the inner sanctuary, to which the only entrance was by way of the outer sanctuary, was the altar of incense, the ark of the covenant, and the mercy seat, the throne of the invisible God. As long as the outer tent remained standing, says the author of *Hebrews*, we were in 'the present age', dealing with earthly things, unable to reach to heavenly things; it was made by human hands and could not change anything in our inner hearts.

The veil between the Holy Place and the Holy of Holies was the one which, according to the gospels, was torn in two at the death of Jesus (Mt 27:51; Mk 15:38; Lk 23:45). The author of *Hebrews* pictures Jesus at that moment moving once and for all into the reality behind the inner sanctuary, namely the presence of God on his mercy seat, Jesus being our high priest for ever. In shedding his blood, he brought it through the veil from the outer sanctuary which was his body 'made by human hands', to where it will be an everlasting sacrifice able to alter our inner selves. He opened the way to heaven itself and the mercy seat, for all of us. 'God wanted all things to be reconciled in him and for him ... when he made peace by his death on the cross' (Col 1:20).

There is a story in *Genesis* of how Abraham pleaded with God to spare the city of Sodom, if he could find fifty just men in the city. When even this proved impossible, Abraham daringly went back to God several times, each time asking for pardon if a smaller number of just men could be found in the city: forty-five, forty, thirty, twenty, ten. When he could not find ten, Abraham lost courage to ask further (Gen 18). A Christian reading the story instinctively wills Abraham to go back yet again and again; for we know that God has spared the whole world, past, present and to come, because there was in it one just man, his own Son Jesus.

But 'this present age', things of the earth, things by human hands, all these must still die, not in sheer destruction, but in order to be transformed into what can live for ever. The movable tent, in which the ark of the covenant stood during tthe journeys of the fathers of the Jewish nation, was transformed into Solomon's temple. That was destroyed at the time of the exile, but a temple was rebuilt on the people's return to Jerusalem. Now in the time of Jesus the temple of Herold the Great was destined for the final destruction, but out of that loss came the indestructible temple, the body and blood of Christ. From the day of Jesus' death, the old temple was bypassed, but by something greater beyond measure.

Jesus talking to the woman at the well of Sychar said, 'Believe me, woman, the hour is coming when you will worship the Father neither on this mountain (where the Samaritans worshipped) nor in Jerusalem . . . The hour is here already when true worshippers will worship the Father in spirit and truth' (Jn 4:21–24). We would say that in our Eucharist we now worship in spirit and truth. Truth is the body of Christ, spirit is the blood of Christ. Truth tells us we are children of God; spirit calls us to give our lives to him in sincere thanks.

A prayer of awe on entering the Holy of Holies

Lord Jesus, you have torn down the veil, and we are standing with you in the presence of the unseen God. To those who have not yet found their way here, you speak encouraging words: 'With confidence draw near to the throne of grace, that you may receive mercy and find grace to help in time of need' (Heb 4:16). It is as if at first you stood outside in the Holy Place, and then the very act of coming through the veil pierced you with a lance and with a thousand wounds, till your Father lifted you up and we were saved. You have told us to keep this precious moment ever before our eyes, in the form of the bread we break and the wine that seems to come from the broken bread. We pray: 'Make our offering acceptable to you, an offering in spirit and in truth'. With your body we stand first in the Holy Place, hearing the words of your truth. With the wine which is your blood we too come through the veil to the inner sanctuary, the place where the innermost core of ourselves can be renewed in spirit by your Father's mercy. Quite simply, we become your sisters and brothers.

But to be able to enter at any time into the most sacred place in the world, which generations and centuries of human beings never dared to approach! No wonder that the price we have to pay is the loss of everything else! Sooner or later, all the glories of the world will desert us whether we are ready or not, but those whom you draw with you into the presence will find again all they have lost, transformed nearly beyond recognition. Just so the old temple was destroyed, but the temple of your body and blood is a thousand times more beautiful. May it be that you will draw to you all men, women and children that ever lived; then no drop of your blood will have been wasted.

Unseen God and Father, I stand before your throne. At first all is dark, or is it that I am dazzled by your nearness? Then my eyes grow used to the dark (or is it the light?) and I see still the golden altar of incense, since the sacrifice of Jesus was lifted up into your presence like incense. I see now the ark of the covenant, your presence with us through all the centuries of our pilgrimage, your watchful care over us through your Son who became one of us. Inside the ark are still the three symbols of your greatest deeds: the rod used by Aaron and Moses, the golden bowl of manna, the stone tablets of the covenant only now they mean for us our escape from sin, the bread of the Eucharist, and the new covenant. You have made all things new, through your Son.

And when I look towards your own self, I see no stranger, but — wonderful to relate — one in whose nature I share, since you chose to be my Father. 'No one knows the Father, except the Son, and those to whom he chooses to reveal him' (Mt 11:27). Jesus has shown you to me, and now there will be others who will know you because, with your strength, I show them. I can only show them what you mean to me, and who you are to me. But I can lead them to Jesus, and he will show them how to find the inner sanctuary in their own hearts in your presence.

But I know only too well that this is only heaven in earth. One day each of us will have to move through the second veil in our own bodies, as we die. Only thus can we follow Jesus our high priest. Then we will possess what now we see as in a glass darkly, and be re-created, receiving back from you what we seemed to leave behind. Then we will know what we already believe, that you have even loved us and pursued us down all the dark ways of our sins.

26

The Way, the Truth and the Life

On the dust-cover of a famous book on the Mass by Fr Joseph Jungmann there is a simple design. It shows a slender cross with wide arms, and no figure upon it; underneath one arm is a loaf of bread, under the other a chalice. The design seemed to me, when I saw it, to picture the saying of Jesus, 'I am the Way, the Truth and the Life' (Jn 14:16). The cross stands for Jesus the Way, the body of Christ in the Eucharist is the Truth, and his blood in the chalice is the Life. Without wanting to limit such a wonderful saying of Jesus to any one meaning, we may still learn something from applying these three words of his to the three images which stand out in Jesus' dying days: the cross, the bread and the wine.

Jesus is the Word of God, and the two words or sayings of his which are repeated at every Eucharist — he himself being the real speaker — are, 'This is my body' and 'This is my blood'. He is undivided, one person. But his words tell us that his body is *here*, his blood *there*. Similarly, there is one Way, which is shown both in his Truth and in his Life which he gives us. 'Faith is the beginning; the end is love'; together they show the Way. We start by believing the truth he brings us, that he himself is Son of God and that God wishes to adopt each one of us as his own daughter or son. We continue, in the strength of that belief, by taking up a life of love, showing to others the love God has first shown us in Christ. The two great commandments of faith and love show the beginning and the end of the Way.

In the outer sanctuary of the temple, the Holy Place, which we have already seen compared to the body of Christ by the author of *Hebrews*, there was 'the lampstand, the table, and the bread of the Presence' (Heb 9:2). The body of Christ is not only 'the bread of the children', it is also a lampstand, a light for the mind. Jesus taught the crowds before he fed them. Readings from scripture, and a homily, have always from the earliest Christian times made up the first part of the Mass. We have even inherited the expression 'the body of doctrine'. Jesus drew the people away from the 'yeast of the Pharisees and the yeast of Herod' (Mk 8:13) so as to teach and feed the people himself. The body of Christ in the Eucharist stands for all God's gifts, of nature and of grace, but our minds need enlightening to see them as gifts, to recognize in ourselves that all life and love and beauty are gifts. And when we do, we are already sharing in the experience of the Son of God. The bread of the Eucharist is the Truth.

The Life is in the chalice: this we have already seen. The most natural meanings of wine as a symbol in the time of Jesus were: blood (and therefore life), and divinity — divine life. As we walk along the Way, having already in us the seed of divine life through believing in Jesus' Good News, the chalice beckons us forward. Whenever death overtakes us, our Father can gather us to himself, but we want him to find us searching for him. We learn to recognize the deep joy, even in times of sorrow, which means he is calling, and to shut our ears to the false joys. We know, having seen the pattern in Christ, that our own death can and will be used by the Father to bring life to some others. We will be a fruitful branch, and the blood of *our* grapes will give life to others, in God's providence.

A prayer to Jesus, the Way, the Truth and the Life

Jesus, the Way, I wish we Christians were still called the Followers of the Way, as in the very early days of your Church (Acts 9:2). Not 'Followers of the Way of Jesus', as if there were other ways besides yours, but Followers of the Way. For there is only one Way, the Way of giving back love in return for love, which is as old as time itself and true outside of time: you are Son of God from all eternity, loving him in return for love. What other way can there be? I wish my eyes, my ears and my heart were so open that I could make my own every word in the scriptures, especially your words to your disciples. Your commands to them were far more in number, and far deeper, that the Ten Commandments our Father gave to Moses. Why, in the gospel of Matthew alone I once counted over fifty commands of yours to those who were with you. But you made things simpler for us. You summed all your wishes up in very few words: 'Do not judge, and you will not be judged' (Mt 7:1); and again, 'Love one another, as I have loved you' (Jn 15:12). Give me the power to do that, Lord Jesus, so that I will follow you along the Way like Bartimaeus (Mk 10:52) and carry your cross, or my cross, with you, like Simon of Cyrene (Mk 15:21).

Jesus, the Truth, help me to tell your voice among the many voices calling for my attention. There is a sweetness in the words that come from you, which nothing and nobody can copy and get away with it for long. Train me to be grateful, to be alert to the endless goodness of your Father to me. Every day, as long as the day is long, he is providing good gifts for me and for the rest of your sisters and brothers, and what do we do? We see only a fraction of the gifts, we fail to see the loving person behind them, we are only intent on the things we are still wanting. Teach me to thank our Father every day, before I ask him for more.

From the beginning of time the waves have been coming and going, and then the trees growing straight and tall, each in their own way loving the Father for his love to them. When you came among us as a man, you gave a voice to all creatures in the universe; you said what they had been trying to find, trying to say since the beginning: 'Abba! Father!' And to us human beings, you gave the gift of saying the same, in truth. You died in that very cause. And you have left with us every day your body, the Truth. How can we praise you enough, except by believing the Truth and setting out along the Way?

Jesus, the Life, we have life the moment we believe in you. But life cannot stand still: it must grow, or die. So it is that every day we need your life to grow within us. We cannot make it grow. Sadly, we can get in the way of its growth. You, however, can make it grow, and you are ever near us. We are not like the knights of long ago who wandered the world looking for the Holy Grail, the chalice you used at the Last Supper. We can come daily to the Eucharist to be built up in your service. When we can receive not only your body but the chalice of your blood, then we see before our eyes the bread that makes us grateful daughters and sons, and the wine that empowers us to love others as a 'thank you' to the Father.

27

The seed grows

We have found in several of these chapters a movement down from God to us, corresponding to the bread of the Eucharist, and a movement back up again from us to God, corresponding to the chalice. How does this double movement show itself in the parables of Jesus about the growth of seeds? 'A sower went out to sow', said Jesus (Mk 4:3); and the seed is the imperishable word of God, 'the good news that was preached to you' (1 Pet 1:23.25). Jesus is the sower, and he sows in us as in Peter the Good News that each of us is either God's daughter or God's son, and for ever. Most of us, again like Peter, take some time to accept the Good News and allow it to take root in ourselves.

For in letting the Good News begin to grow in us, we have to go through a form of death. Once I am God's son or his daughter, the answer to the question 'Who am I?' becomes 'I am So-on-So, God's son/daughter'. So it was that John in his gospel never called himself John, but 'the disciple Jesus loved'. Everyone who reads his gospel is invited to take that title to himself or herself, and to become simply 'the disciple Jesus loves'. That is my glory; that is more important than battles I have won, mountains I have scaled, cities I have built. I have to let go of everything I thought most precious about myself, and prize only God's unshakable love for me. Then when battles are lost, or mountains or cities destroyed, I can still say 'I am God's child' and my heart is founded on everlasting rock; nothing changes.

The sowing, then, and the taking root of the seed correspond to the giving of the bread of the Eucharist and the faith with which we receive it as the sign of God's unfailing love for us. From then on, the seed begins to grow, and it is the chalice which gives us the correct image. If as Jesus takes root in us he says 'This is my body', then equally as his life begins to grow and develop in us the word he says is 'This is my blood'. The roots continue to push down deeper and fill our nothingness with God, but the plant breaks out into the open air, grows quietly, resists all its enemies, and finally becomes fruitful.

By ourselves and apart from the fatherhood of God, what we do is based on the wrong answer to the question 'Who am I?'. We can only do lasting good under the inspiration of God's Spirit: actions done in the power of that Spirit are completely rooted and founded in love, done without fear of losing that love. God for his part can do only good; the nearest he can come to doing evil is when we do evil and he in his humility and hope for us goes along with what we do, giving us life and strength. Such is the difference between us. As we drink the chalice of love after having taken the bread of God's love for us, we are inspired and moved towards doing good. The fruits of the Spirit are 'love, joy, peace, patience, kindness, goodness, trustfulness, gentleness and self-control' (Gal 5:22) lasting all through life and into death. Under the branches of a plant with such fruits, birds find shelter (Mk 4:32). Such fruits carry the good news of God's fatherly love to another generation of seekers: this is the thirty-fold, the sixty-fold, the hundredfold increase promised by Jesus (Mk 4:8).

Jesus implied that some of his enemies (or was it just blind humanity?) had the spirit of evil for a father (Jn 8:44). 'You will be able to tell them by their fruits' (Mt 7:20).

Prayer of one who desires to grow

Father of unfailing love, 'our help and guide, make your love the root of our lives. May our love for you express itself in our eagerness to do good for others" (cf. Prayer, Week 28 of the Year). Well I know that my actions are very mixed between good and evil. When I see myself drifting further from the kind of life I wish in my heart of hearts to live, let me not attempt to double my efforts, because such strength is only my own, and is bound to fail in time. Let me rather return to my roots, and find healing in your constant fatherly love. The more I know myself loved, the more good I shall do.

Be the gardener to my plant, whether we call it a wheat plant, or a vine, or an olive tree. You did not create us evil. If only you adopt and prune us, we shall produce good fruit. If we produce sour grapes, it can only be because we have kept you from our vineyard too long.

I know that you love me as your son, and as if I were your only child; you love me whether I am tall or short, dark or fair, black or white, clever or slow, gifted or dull, successful or a failure, warm and loving towards you or cold and distant. My maker puts no conditions on his love: he loves me because he loves me! Given such a security, how can I fail to respond? Your love is like a cool rain soothing me in time of trouble, and like a warm air encouraging me to grow, when I feel stronger. You fill my days with hopeful sunshine, and take away the self-reproach that comes at night-time, for with you all is forgiven, from end to end of time.

Lord Jesus, life of my life, I can only tell you of my desires as I remember your word-pictures. I desire to be like a sound olive tree, bringing oil to heal and strengthen and nourish mankind. I desire to be like a good vine in a good vineyard, bringing people the grape to eat and the blood of the grape to drink. I desire to be like a good fig tree in the vineyard, with fruit to offer at any time you come looking for fruit. I wonder was the tree of life ever thought to be a fig tree (Gen 3:7)? In any case, I would desire to be part with you in the tree of life, bringing your life to all peoples and nations. I desire to be like good corn, growing straight and plentiful, to feed those who are hungry. I desire to be like the mustard plant, sheltering your little ones in my shade and telling them of your Father's great love. All these fruits die to themselves in becoming useful to others; but I have already died to myself in becoming 'the one my Father loves'. That was his gift rather than my sacrifice, and I trust that my physical death when it comes will also turn out to be a gift.

These then are my desires, Jesus my brother, and I pray you to drive my growth in the direction of my desires, by your living blood which you share with me. 'This is my blood', you say, and your blood, your love, urges us in the direction of unselfishness. At times in my life nothing much seems to be happening. I pray that at such times the seed may be growing secretly, 'first the blade, then the ear, then the full grain in the ear'. Give me, please, the patience of your own hidden years, so that in the end I may give full glory, in you, to the Father.

H

28
Goodness and power

'And as Jesus was setting out on his way, a man ran up and knelt before him and asked him, "Good Master, what must I do to inherit eternal life?" ' Before Jesus answered the man's question, he replied with another question: 'Why do you call me good? No one is good but God alone' (Mk 10:17f). 'Goodness' is a word in the gospels that has a direct link with the chalice, and with the body of Christ once the blood has been shed, since goodness is divine, something to be found only in God. The shepherd is known to be good when he lays down his life for his sheep (Jn 10:11). He is doing as God would do, and can only be doing it under the inspiration of God's Spirit. The good Samaritan we call good because that kind of selflessness is found only where God is. There is in parents, who could even be otherwise evil, nearly always enough goodness to give only good gifts to their children; so most surely will God give his Spirit to his children who ask him (cf. Lk 11:13).

Good seed in good soil, good plants and trees yield up their fruit in good measure. By their fruits we are to know them. And only the good self-sacrificing plant or tree gives up its fruit to the hungry, the thirsty and those with no money. There is a passage in *Hebrews* in which the author reminds his readers of the process by which they were initiated into the Christian way. They were 'enlightened' (a word which reminds us of Baptism); they have tasted the heavenly gift (which sounds like the Eucharist under the form of bread, rather as Jesus fed the crowds); they have become partakers of the Holy Spirit (which may remind us of the transfiguration of Jesus, or the sacrament we call Confirmation, or the 'active' side of Baptism); lastly, they have tasted the goodness of the word of God and the powers of the age to come (cf. Heb 6:4f). If 'the goodness of the word of God' refers to the body of Christ, surely 'the powers of the age to come' refers to the blood of Christ. The 'word of God' would then mean especially the Lord's words, 'This is my body; this is my blood'. So St Irenaeus a century later would say, 'The mingled chalice and the bread made by hands receive the word of God' (*Against Heresies*, V 2:3). The word of God like a sharp sword divides blood from body in Christ.

*   *   *

We have seen already that 'the age to come' and the chalice are connected. So too the notion of 'power' is closely linked with the chalice. 'Power', along with 'clouds' and 'glory' and 'angels', is a word used to describe the coming of the Son of Man. Jesus often referred to himself as the Son of Man when prophesying his coming passion. Once Jesus turns his face firmly towards Jerusalem, these words and ideas keep cropping up: *power, able, unable, possible, impossible, can, cannot, weak.*

This is so especially in Mark's gospel. The kingdom of God will come with power; (a cloud overshadows Jesus and the three apostles on the mountain;) the epileptic boy cannot speak; the boy's father appeals to Jesus, 'If you can, have pity'; Jesus replies, 'All things are possible to him who believes'; the disciples could not heal him, for they had not prayed; children were praised (as showing true power and authority?); with God's power it is possible for a rich man to enter the kingdom; 'Can you drink my chalice?'; the fig tree can provide no fruit, nor for that matter can the temple; the Sadducees do not understand the power of God in the resurrection; the woman at Bethany did what she could in anointing Jesus. Jesus felt weak in the Garden but he prayed, and was able to speak up and say who he was at his trial. Hence his death was fruitful. Peter was weak at that time, and did not pray for power, so was unable to speak up on trial by the fire.

The power is the power to let the divine blood in me speak out when I am on trial. The glory comes from the Father in the resurrection.

A prayer to our good Father

Father of goodness, all created goodness comes from you as sunbeams come from the sun or as rivers flow down from their source. If there is anything good in me, it comes from you. You formed me long ago, and gave me love and faithfulness through my parents and through those who loved me and taught me in my early days, and those who have loved or befriended me through all my life, and through all those who work continually to keep together the world around me. Like every other sinner on this earth, I have received from you far more than I have given in return. All praise to you, and all thanks, for your gifts. I have not even mentioned the sun, the moon, the stars, all the plants and animals of which you have made us stewards. They are so full of beauty, and so patient, like the rocks and the ground under our feet.

Your Son Jesus taught us to see all these as good gifts from you, with yourself, and the Spirit, and himself as your greatest gift. Help us now, by this chalice of his blood, to grow fruitful and to give your goodness to others. Let my every breathing-in be a 'please', asking for your goodness to continue; let my every breathing-out be a 'thank you' to you, shown in goodness to my sisters and brothers. Your goodness has been poured into me for so many years; let me learn to open my doors and share your goodness with others, especially those who otherwise cannot believe in your goodness. Transfigure me so that others can look at me and see your glory transfiguring a sinner.

A prayer to the Son of Man

Lord Jesus, Son of Man, how is it that I can praise God as my Father, speaking to him, but when I try to speak of him before men as my Father, the words are so often plucked from my mouth? Increase my little faith. Always let that be my prayer: increase the little faith I have. My spirit is willing, but my flesh is weak; as long as I am in this physical body, strengthen my weak flesh so that I can show the true face of my Father to those among whom he has sent me. The good I want to do, I cannot do; the evil I do not want to do, this is sometimes all I can do. Nor can I free the tongues of others to speak God's praises, unless he gives me power as he gave you power.

And the power to let go of my talents and other riches and to give them to the poor, this too I ask for in your name. I want to be like a little child, with no power of its own except to ask, and to have the stubborn ways of a child, to ask and ask until it receives. Please grant me to take your chalice and drink it, for in that chalice is the power God gave you to give to us. I believe in the power of God to join us to you as you come in glory on the clouds of heaven with the holy angels.

The Son of Man ushers in the kingdom of God and his everlasting reign (cf. Dan 7). The kingdom of God is where forgiveness reigns. Forgive our shortcomings: do not be ashamed of us when you come. We are given one glimpse of God's loveliness and we think our journey is over. Give us the humility to pray and to keep on praying, as long as we are in this frail flesh. Faith does not stop growing at our Baptism, but must grow continually by your gift and the gift of your Father, to be the root and ground of our loving, until the day when faith is no more and there is only love left.

29

The story of Joseph

The famous story of Joseph is told in the last fourteen chapters of the book of *Genesis*. In the course of the story Joseph's many brothers go down from the land of Canaan into Egypt to trade for corn, since there is a famine in both lands, but there is plenty of corn stored in Egypt. What they find in Egypt turns out to be so much more than just corn, and it is this 'so much more' which can be used to picture what the wine of the Eucharist adds in meaning to the bread, made from corn by human hands, of the Eucharist.

Joseph was the favourite son of Jacob his father. A father should not really have favourites. God our Father has no favourites either according to both St Peter (Acts 10.34) and St Paul (Rom 2:11), except in the sense that every child of his is unique in his eyes and therefore in that sense a favourite, no less and no more than all the others. But Jacob let it be seen that he loved Joseph, the first son of his favourite wife, more than his other sons and daughters. Joseph's brothers became jealous, especially when he told them he had dreamt they were all, and his parents too, bowing down respectfully to him. The gift of a special coat from Jacob to Joseph was the last straw. The brothers seized an opportunity that offered, and cast Joseph down a dry well to die. Later they relented, at the suggestion of Reuben (as one version has it) or of Judah (according to another version). They sold him into slavery in Egypt. His coat they covered in goat's blood and sent back to his father, leaving him to surmise in his grief that some wild beast had killed his dearest son.

Joseph suffered the desolation of being first of all left down the well to die, then of being sold into slavery by his brothers. As a slave to Potiphar, commander of the king's guard in Egypt, he quickly gained his master's trust but was then falsely accused by his master's wife, ending up in prison. In prison he again quickly advanced to a position of trust, where he was able to help another prisoner who was released and who put in a good word for Joseph. After Joseph was himself released to interpret Pharaoh's dreams, he rose to become the Pharaoh's right hand man, his vizier or the governor of the land. Joseph's foresight prepared the land of Egypt to survive the coming years of famine, while at the same time he greatly increased the royal power.

When the famine hit the land of Canaan, Jacob sent his sons to buy corn from Egypt. They went for corn, and eventually found not only corn but free corn, not only free corn but a feast, not only a feast but their brother, not a vengeful brother but a forgiving one, one willing to share with them and with their families the immense good fortune into which he had come. He brought them all, and their parents and their wives and children and servants, to live in comfort under his protection in Egypt.

Before Joseph told the brothers who he was, he played cat-and-mouse with them for some time in what we see as hardly a Christian manner! For instance, he made them go and fetch young Benjamin, his only full brother, from Canaan and then hid his own chalice in Benjamin's purchases, to make him seem a thief. The story makes the brothers say at this stage, 'Truly we are being called to account for our brother Joseph. We saw his misery of soul ... but we did not listen to him and now this misery has come home to us' (Gen 42:21).

Joseph's forgiveness when it came was complete. It survived even their father's death, when the brothers took fright, fearing Joseph would now take his revenge. Instead, Joseph kept them in his favour, showing that his love for them was his own, not just for their father's sake. He said to them, 'Do not be afraid; is it for me to put myself in God's place?'

Praise for a brother who forgives

Jesus, my brother, how many details in this story of Joseph and his brothers remind me of the way things stand between you and me! You had every right to be called our Father's favourite Son, since we are only sons and daughters of his by adoption. And your dreams drove your brothers to madness, as when you said at your trial, 'Yes, I am the Son of the Blessed One, and you will see the Son of Man seated at the right hand of the Power and coming with the clouds of heaven' (Mk 14:62).

So too when it comes to wondering which of the brothers of Joseph was most to blame for his death. Descendants of Reuben and of Judah wanted to lessen the blame upon themselves, and told the story accordingly: Reuben or Judah brought it about that Joseph stayed alive, though their father was never likely to know he was still alive. All Jacob had was a bloodstained coat, the coat which had been a special gift to his son Joseph. The father mourned, with a mourning that would, he thought, last as long as his life. All the brothers consented to that. We may argue about who was most to blame for your death, Jesus, but not one of us had power to stop it happening. No mere human being had that power. Your Father trusted you to our human weakness, and we put you on a cross. Your mother did not receive your bloodstained clothes; the soldiers divided those. She received your own body, stained with its own blood.

Joseph's brothers came to buy corn, and found not only free corn but a forgiving brother. Joseph in Egypt is very like you in your resurrection. You give us an abundance of corn without our having to pay the price at all — your own body in the bread of the Eucharist. With it you give us not simply water, which we need, but an abundance of new wine as well. We sit down with you as at a banquet and we recognize you now at the breaking of bread (Lk 24:35). Joseph singled out Benjamin, his own full brother, for special favours but also for special trials, as when he put his own silver cup in Benjamin's sack of corn, to make it look as if Benjamin had stolen it. You, Jesus, have the same total love for each of us as your Father has. With you there are no favourites — every sister and every brother is a favourite. And you share with us your chalice, though we feel a little like thieves when we first take it, since this is a royal banquet and we feel ourselves unlikely guests.

Like Joseph you offer us a royal way of life, the special protection of the Most High King, and a complete reunion with all those of our family whom we grieve for. Like Joseph and Pharaoh, you and our heavenly Father tell us to leave our property behind, to bring only ourselves, since there is plenty in the land we are destined for (Gen 45:20). Like Joseph you say, 'The evil you planned to do me has by God's design been turned to good, that he might bring about, as indeed he has, the deliverance of a numerous people. So you need not be afraid; I myself will provide for you and your descendants' (Gen 50:19ff). The way you turn our murder of you into a blessing upon us is so swift and so wonderful. And such a blessing, so many blessings!

30

The scapegoat

'Aaron must lay his hands on the head of the other goat, and confess all the faults of the sons of Israel, all their transgressions and all their sins, and lay them to its charge. Having thus laid them on the goat's head, he shall send it out into the desert . . . and the goat will bear all their faults away with it into a desert place' (Lev 16:21f). There we have the picture of the scapegoat, a figure which has often been applied to Jesus in his suffering. Between the early days of Moses and Aaron and the fullness of time in Jesus, comes the prophetic figure of the Suffering Servant of Yahweh, who makes the link between the scapegoat and Jesus: 'And yet ours were the sufferings he bore, ours the sorrows he carried. But we, we thought of him as someone punished, struck by God, and brought low. Yet he was pierced through for our faults, crushed for our sins. On him lies a punishment that brings us peace, and through his wounds we are healed . . . Yahweh burdened him with the sins of all of us. Harshly dealt with, he bore it humbly, he never opened his mouth' (cf. Is 53:4–7).

Over the head of Jesus when he was crucified was fixed the notice of his supposed crime: 'Jesus of Nazareth, King of the Jews'. St Paul implies that the real crimes he was dying for were ours; our crimes were nailed above his head and in his death he took them away with him, after which they were never seen or mentioned again (cf. Col 2:14).

In the Old Testament, the cup of wine sometimes stands for the anger of God 'God, you have been angry . . . you have allowed your people to suffer, to drink a wine that makes us reel' (Ps 59[60]:1–3). Yahweh is holding a cup of frothing wine, heavily drugged, that the wicked must all drain to the dregs (cf. Ps 74[75]:8). We could say that Jesus in his death took all the anger of God as it is depicted in the Old Testament, took it upon himself, took it with him into the desert in which he died, and left us instead with the true vision of God, whom each and every one of us, from the greatest to the least, may truly call 'my Father'. Jesus is the passover kid, as well as the passover lamb (cf. Ex 12:5).

God was not angry with Jesus, nor was he even angry with us. The picture of God which the Old Testament often gives us is of an angry God. But as we have seen, Jesus is only distressed over those who judge others, and with those who try to fix a price on God's mercy. The God whom Jesus shows us is a God who forgives endlessly those who will accept his forgiveness, if they will in their turn show mercy to others. It was an act of tremendous courage, for Jesus alone as he had to be, to take all the centuries of accumulated guilt and to say human beings need carry it no longer. 'Sufferings are not punishment, any more than earthly blessings are always a sign of God's approval.' Like a good slave with his master, Jesus gave thanks to God for all blessings, but did not blame God when he had to suffer.

Prayer of one who is alone

Jesus, scapegoat for my sins, you were the first to teach the world to call God 'my Father', 'my own Father'. So too you were the first to carry the duty of telling sinners not to fret over past sins, since their Father had already forgiven them. Such was the uproar your message caused, I wonder if even you sometimes feared you had been too bold? But no, I think your certainty was too great for you ever to be in doubt. But you must certainly have felt very much alone, when even your closest three disciples, Peter, James and John, slept through your hour of greatest need. *Gethsemane* is well named, meaning as it does 'a place where olives are crushed'. The oil which came from that night's work is for our healing.

You know the picture, Jesus, in the museum near here, of the scapegoat in the salt desert; and you know how I speak to you when I see it. For in me also there is a deep sense of being alone at times, as there is in every human being. My aloneness is never complete loneliness, since I know you are in the desert with me. I hope you in your heart knew the presence of your Father. Is there any way, Master, in which my being alone can be of service to you? As you use my hands and my tongue and my heart, can you also use my loneliness and make it your own? What must I do, to find you in the desert and join my loneliness to yours? I suppose I can say with the Good Thief, 'I am getting no more (or not much more) than I deserve, whereas you have no reason at all to be out here in the desert!' I suppose I can try to live an innocent life, so as even late in the day to become more like you. And if you give me the vision, I can, like you, conceal my sonship, my divine sonship, and see things like a slave. With the Suffering Servant, I will say 'thank you' to my Father for all his endless gifts, but I shall not open my mouth about my sufferngs. Why should I, once I know they are not to be looked on as punishments any more? What they are, where they come from is often a mystery, but once I know they are not signs of God's displeasure, I am content.

The sight of you out there in the salt, white, desert near the Dead Sea gives me another thought. You look to me like one of the meek who will inherit the land (Mt 5:4). The world shares out its plentiful goods, and gives the salt desert to the scapegoat. 'That's your share. Consider yourself lucky.' You could have made war — heaven knows, you had thousands of keen followers. But you let them squeeze you out. 'Fair enough,' you said, 'I'll have the desert, you have the fertile land.' Yet the hearts of the greedy were not satisfied, whereas you as the Son of the Most High who owns both desert and fertile land, you inherited both, desert and fertile land alike. What we lose willingly for your sake, we gain for ever. Teach me how to do the same, and to understand that this is not a selfish exercise. If you and I are willing to share our inheritance on these unequal terms with our brothers and sisters, then perhaps the Father will change all hearts before the kingdom is fully revealed. You alone did this for all the rest of mankind. You can continue to do it through me, whenever I feel overlooked or badly done by.

Most of all, my brother, my leader, I thank you for drinking the cup first, before you gave it to me to drink, and for showing by your death and resurrection that the cup is not filled with God's anger, but with a Father's love for his guilty children. We could say, you drank the cup of the anger of the old covenant, drank it to the dregs; then you gave us instead a new wine to drink. 'See,' you said, so gently, 'I take out of your hand the cup of stupor, the chalice of my wrath; you shall drink it no longer' (Is 51:22).

110

31

The seven last words

Taking the four gospels together, we find the evangelists have recorded seven sayings of Jesus from the cross, which are traditionally known as 'The seven last words'. Each from his own point of view, Matthew, Mark, Luke and John shows us in these sayings what he sees as the last words of Jesus. Mankind has always found special truth and complete sincerity in anyone's dying words, spoken when there is no longer anything to be gained by concealment. How much more, then, the dying words of Jesus are for us the parting messages of our elder brother, bringing us back to the things that really matter. The words will have special meaning for us as we receive the chalice of his blood, since these are the words he spoke as he shed that blood for us. His blood in our veins will always want to be saying these very words, or words very like them.

'Father, forgive them; they do not know what they are doing' (Lk 23:34). Not 'Father, forgive them if they stop killing me'; not 'Father, forgive them if they promise never to do it again'. But 'Father, forgive them; they do not know what they are doing'. Of course in one way, they knew very well what they were doing; but truly they did not know what it really was they were doing. Do I pray like that for my enemies?

'Indeed, I promise you,' said Jesus to the thief, 'today you will be with me in paradise' (Lk 23:43). Do I make the entry into paradise seem so easy to poor broken human beings who are dying? This thief acknowledged his own guilt, and refused to judge Jesus for not setting him free. No more than that, but, says Jesus, it is enough. 'Judge not, and you will not be judged.'

Seeing his mother and the disciple he loved standing near her, Jesus said to his mother, 'Woman, this is your son'. Then to the disciple he said, 'This is your mother' (Jn 19:26). How high on my priorities does it stand, to say to each and every disciple, each one of whom is 'the disciple Jesus loves', that Mary is his or her mother? How often do I remind Mary that each one of them is her own child, especially when they are in need?

'I am thirsty' (Jn 19:28). Now that I know the glory that is in the chalice, why do I not speak of my thirst for it more often, even though the only response from the world at large might be to offer me vinegar, sour grapes?

'My God, my God, why have you forsaken me?' (e.g., Mk 15:34). Jesus quotes the first line of Psalm 22[23]. When I feel forsaken, do I *tell God* so, even using the formal 'my God' instead of 'my Father' because I feel distanced from him?

'It is accomplished' (Jn 19:30). Even the Good Thief could have said the same, such is the power of God to take up and transform even a sinful life by the light of his own mercy — the greater the sinner, the greater the mercy. At the end of my days, I should say the same. Do I say it each night, before each little death of sleep?

'Father, into your hands I commend my spirit' (Lk 23:46). Again Jesus quotes from a psalm (Psalm 31[32]:5) but now he has found himself again, and he reverts to his habit of calling God 'Abba', even though the psalm itself there calls him 'Yahweh'. The Church's Night Prayer gives us the same words as the refrain of our night prayer, every night.

Lastly, Mark tells us Jesus gave a loud cry of victory and died (Mk 15:38).

Prayers from the heart

Mary, my Mother, I need you. Now that all my body and all my psyche belongs to Jesus, my new flesh needs a new mother, one like you alone in whom the empire of sin has never set foot. Teach me how to grow, in patience.

And when Jesus was dying, he seems to have felt forsaken by his beloved Abba for a short time. I have known someone who was, you would say, goodness and motherliness itself in her lifetime, yet when her death came near she was frightened, feeling strongly that she would die and that would be that. Her body and soul cried out against the threat of extinction. In the hour of our death, pray for us sinners, your children. Stand by us as you stood by your Son. Help

112

us to say to ourselves, 'Even if this is the end of all, I would rather have done as I did, trying to live by the values of Jesus, than to have lived a life of greed'.

Jesus, my Way, along with you on the cross I forgive yet again all my enemies, all those I have disapproved of, all those I have hurt in any way great or small. They did not know what they were doing. They did not know that I am as dear to your Father as if I were his only son, or they would never have judged me. They meant well; they thought I was a threat to them or to the values they held dear, perhaps even for your sake or your Father's sake! Take from me my judge's robes and my judge's wig! I acquit them all before I come to you. This judge resigns from the bench.

I am thirsty for your new wine. Let it not matter to me that so often I find only sour grapes offered to me, since you have given me your new wine, and that is more than enough for me. The vinegar in my life I accept as the scapegoat did, in hopes that if I have drunk some, perhaps some person who is unhappy may then have less of it to drink; or they may even be able to learn from me, through you, that vinegar is not a sign of God's disfavour.

At the end of my days, at the end of each day, I say 'It is over. Thanks be to God!' May I one day share in your cry of triumph as you tore apart the veil before the Holy of Holies, body and soul as well as spirit.

Father, my Father, you give me the invitation to say to all poor sinners who turn to you, 'This day we shall be together in paradise'. With you, a thousand years is but a day, and the sun is already risen on the day of the Lord. This night and every night and at the hour of my death, Father, I hand over my breathing to you, since it is yours. And in the meantime I ask of you the gift that Jesus evidently had, of making my own all the prayers of scripture. When I go into my room and shut the door as Jesus told us to, then I am alone with you. No one else comes in then unless we want them to. Why should I be afraid of being overheard, in secret there with you? There, for that time, is the Holy of Holies; for that time, I am as it were the one and only high priest, by courtesy of your Son — that is to say, I am then a little child alone with its Father.

32
Precious stones

The time has come to return, as promised, to the image of 'precious stones'. The word 'precious' alerts me to the fact that we are in the realm of the precious blood of Jesus. Peter, called the Rock, or the Stone, by Jesus, writes to his readers 'Come to Jesus, to that living stone, rejected by men but in God's sight chosen and precious; and like living stones be yourselves built into a *spirit*ual house ... For it stands in scripture "Behold, I am laying in Zion a stone, a corner-stone chosen and precious; and he who believes in him will not be put to shame". To you, therefore, who believe, he is precious, but for those who do not believe, "The very stone which the builders rejected has become the head of the corner" ' (1 Pet 2:4–7). Peter is quoting first of all from Isaiah, and then from Psalm 117[118]. That second quotation, about the stone rejected by the builders, is only to be found in the New Testament in places traditionally associated with Peter: in Mark (12:10f), which is the gospel most likely to be directly connected with Peter, in Matthew and Luke where they adopt the same passage of Mark into their own gospels, and in a speech of Peter in Acts (4:11), and in the Letter of Peter just quoted.

Peter was present, and deeply interested, when Jesus said about the temple, 'Do you see these great buildings?' Someone had just exclaimed 'Look, Teacher, what wonderful stones and what wonderful buildings!' Jesus went on, 'There will not be left here one stone upon another, that will not be thrown down' (cf. Mk 13:1–3). Just as the promising-looking fig tree has been found fruitless, so too the temple is fruitless, at least in its inability to provide fruit on demand, at any season, when the owner's son comes looking for fruit. The temple, after all, is only from the earth. This temple, and all human temples, is bound to fail, as is the very earth itself, when it would reach up to heaven with an unfailing ladder.

The Fathers of the early Church dwell at some length on the

symbolic fact that the altars of the temples in Jerusalem (of Solomon, of Ezra's time, of Herod the Great) like the altar ordered to be built by Moses (cf. 20:25), were not chiselled or cut by human hands, but their stones were taken undressed, and this by divine command (cf. 1 Macc 4:47 and Dan 2:34.45). Again we are in the domain of the blood of Christ, in the view of the Fathers (e.g., Justin, *Trypho*, 75).

The new Jerusalem comes down from heaven, not up from earth. It has twelve foundation stones, standing for the twelve apostles of the Lamb, and also corresponding to the twelve months of the year, each of them fruitful. For the foundation stones are each adorned with a different kind of jewel, and those twelve jewels or semi-precious stones are the traditional stones of the signs of the zodiac (as William Barclay pointed out). Here is the list. We notice that for John, a Jew of his own time and place, the year began with the month of March, but for some reason his list marches *backwards* up the months of the year, starting with February, then January, December, November and so on, back up to March. Perhaps he wanted to put Peter the fisherman in first place? The list of stones as it appears in John's *Revelation* (chapter 21) is thus: 1. diamond (Pisces); 2. lapis lazuli (Aquarius); 3. turquoise (Capricorn); 4. crystal (Sagittarius): 5. agate (Scorpio); 6. ruby (Libra); 7. gold quartz (Virgo); 8. malachite (Leo); 9. topaz (Cancer); 10. emerald (Gemini); 11. sapphire (Taurus); 12. amethyst (Aries). The first shall be last, and the last first. Each of them is fruitful (this is the land of the tree of life), and each is precious, though each is different.

A prayer of love for beauty

'Beauty so ancient and so new', my Father, all the beauty of this world, and of the new heaven and the new earth, comes from you. The sun is like gold; the moon is like silver; the stars are like diamonds and precious stones and pearls. The astronomers tell us the stars are disappearing beyond our ken faster than they could ever count them. Yet each star has its own spectrum, its own particular range of colours, its own version of the rainbow, just as surely as every human being has a personal thumb-print. And the scriptures tell us, you call each of the stars by name: they are precious in your eyes, just as each of us your children is precious to you. I would not

115

I

exchange my place in the wheeling of the stars for any other: I have but one place in your heart, and that is enough for me, because there I have no rivals. I could conquer the world like Alexander, and still earn no greater position in the scheme of things. So why need my heart be restless, ever again?

I have watched bricklayers at work. They go round the foundations with the first layers of bricks. They come to, say, waist level, and my eyes fasten on one particular brick. There it sits, open to the sky, fair and square on top of two other bricks, half its weight on each. And yet the two parent bricks are themselves dependent on the layers underneath, and on their neighbour bricks, and above all on the foundations, without which the strain on the mortar would be excessive. Meanwhile my particular brick, on what is at present the top row, is at ease and presumably thinks all bricks were designed to serve it.

But then, all too soon for my particular brick, the bricklayer comes round again, and puts another row on top, and another on top of that. My brick feels the strain, but if the architect has done his designs right, the strain will not be more than the brick can bear.

In other words, each of us is born a child of two human parents (except for your Son, our chief foundation stone), is spoiled for a little while and then takes its place in the community, sharing or carrying the burdens of others. Your Son is the rock upon whom we all rest, for he brings us your everlasting, unshakable love. He gave his precious blood to be our most precious stone, he the stone not cut from the Rock by any human hands. You yourself are the Rock, my rock, my fortress, my stronghold.

May our house be a *spiritual* house, a house built on his foundation. At the end of the Sermon on the Mount in Matthew (7:24–27), as at the end of the Sermon on the Plain in Luke (6:47ff), Jesus tells us that the one who builds his house on rock is the one who comes to him and listens to his words and acts on them. 'Believe that Yahweh is your beloved *"Abba"* as he is mine: trust him. Then turn no jealous eye on anyone else; judge nobody.' Jesus let himself be rejected by men, so as to bring that utterly firm reassurance to me and to the rest of us sinners. How can we ever thank you, and him, and the Spirit, for rebuilding our shattered hearts on such a firm foundation of love?

'You have made us for yourself, beauty so ancient and so new, and our heart is restless until it finds rest in you.' Most of us can add, as St Augustine does himself, 'Late have I loved thee'. But how much better late than never!

33

My city, my kingdom

The new Jerusalem comes down from heaven, so once again we are in the region of the blood of Christ.

The heavenly Jerusalem as described in John's *Revelation* (chapters 21 and 22) bears a remarkable resemblance to the city of Babylon as it was in the time of the exile of the Jewish people (590–538 B.C.). Probably the sheer size, power and physical beauty of that city stayed vividly in the communal memory of those who returned to rebuild Jerusalem. For his description John would seem to rely on the description of Babylon in its heyday by the Greek historian Herodotus (volume I, 178–200). Present-day archaeologists find inaccuracies in Herodotus' description, but while John was no twentieth-century archaeologist, he was a skilled writer of the Greek language, living in a Greek culture in Asia Minor, where the histories of Herodotus would surely be available to a man of letters.

Old Babylon, Herodotus tells us, was a square city: the city walls formed a square in shape, each wall being 120 stadia long. The new Jerusalem, John tells us, is a square city: each wall is 12,000 stadia (1,500 miles) long, or a hundred times the length of the old Babylon's walls. The area of the new Jerusalem is therefore 10,000 times that of the old Babylon. Anything earth can do, God can do better, ten thousand times better.

Then comes what at first sounds an odd statistic — the height of the heavenly city is the same as the length of one of its sides. Does that mean the city is a perfect cube, like some unthinkably huge modern office block? No. The building in old Babylon which was as tall as it was long as it was broad, was the temple of Marduk, the *ziggurat* already well known to us as the Tower of Babel (Gen 11). The shape is not cubic, but, roughly speaking, a pyramid. It consists of 8 storeys of diminishing area the higher they got, though each storey was of the same consistent height. Modern archaeologists tell us this, not Herodotus. The total height of the *ziggurat* was the same as the length, or the breadth, of a side of the ground floor: 90 metres. What John has done is to superimpose the images of city and temple. The city is the temple. 8 storeys, 7 stairways.

Back to Herodotus. Old Babylon had a moat. Empty the moat and look at the walls from outside. The foundations of the city walls are revealed where the moat waters were, under ground level. The city walls as such are above ground level. In the heavenly Jerusalem John puts the twelve apostles as the foundations of the walls, the twelve patriarchs of Israel as the walls. Next, the river. In the old Babylon, the River Euphrates flowed down straight through the middle of the city, cutting it into two equal rectangles. The river is broad, making a broadway, and the city's streets are all straight and all intersect at right angles, running either parallel to the river or at right angles to it. In the heavenly Jerusalem the same, except that for John the river has its source within the city and *then* flows down in a broadway. (For Ezekiel the river starts under the temple and flows north, south, east and west, like the rivers of Eden — see Ezek 40.) Like Zion, the new Jerusalem must have its own source of living (i.e., fresh) water.

In old Babylon, the rectangle on one side of the river had for its focal point the royal palace. The other rectangle had for its focal point the *ziggurat*, the temple of Marduk, the tower of Babel, meaning 'Gateway of the gods', rather than 'confusion' as the author of Genesis sees it. The people of Babylon were descended from mountain-dwellers of the north. In the old days they had found divinity, and therefore worshipped, on mountain tops. Down here in the fertile plain they had no mountains, so they built their *ziggurats* mountain-shaped, out of bricks made by human hands out of the clay of the earth. Herodotus tells us that on the summit of the *ziggurat* no human being ever passed the night except one native woman (for other ceremonies strangers were required) 'chosen by the god out of the whole nation, as the Chaldeans, who are priests of this deity, say'. This much Herodotus credits, but not what the priests also say, that the deity visits her as she reclines on the bed, shut up in the temple on the topmost storey. The new Jerusalem is the bride. The purpose of the marriage in the new Jerusalem is not, as it probably was in Babylon, to bend the will of the god to human ambitions, but to unite the human will to God's. Jesus was very upset when the temple of Jerusalem was being used as a short-cut (Mk 11:16). For New Testament writers, the new Jerusalem is a ladder to God, but on God's terms. And it means the opposite of 'confusion'.

In Luke's gospel, in Jesus' parable of the pounds, the newly-crowned king gives to the man who did well with the ten pounds, ten cities as a reward (Lk 19:17). Ten cities, a whole province, like the Decapolis region. John in *Revelation* goes even further, saying we will all be kings (4:9f), and will reign for ever (22:5). In more exact terms, perhaps, when we take the whole Old and New Testament into account, we will be princes and princesses, each with our own principality. God our Father is the king, who invites us to his son's wedding banquet, we being younger brothers and sisters of the first-born (cf. especially Mt 22:1). Christ is king under God his Father. Christ's crown while on earth was a crown of thorns, his royal robe his own blood, alas.

Alan T. Dale, who translated the Old and New Testament into English that would be directly understood by young people unfamiliar with biblical language and imagery, translates 'the kingdom of God' as 'living in God's way'. Where God is king, things are done in certain ways and not in other ways: trust is the first law, forgiveness the second, and so on. God's way is to call himself our Father, and to send his Son with the message that he will adopt us all.

So whatever else it means, to say that each of us will be an independent prince or princess, it does not mean that we will rule each other, nor shall we rule any other of God's free creatures. We may now be stewards for a time, but never rulers.

Then what is there left to rule? Where will be my own principality, my own kingdom? 'The kingdom of heaven is within you', replies Jesus (cf. Lk 17:21; Mt 3:2). To use a trivial example as an illustration of what is, I think, a deep truth, life is like a game of Ludo. We each have our own viewpoint, our own corner, our own colour, our own counters; and the game, which we all share equally, matters more than 'who wins?' Heaven and earth and all they contain are as much mine as they are yours, by the gift of God, so long as we do not try to rule and possess them, so long as we do not have ambition to win against others. What I am asked to rule is my own *psyche* and my own body, that is to say my own 'flesh'. With God's power I can slowly come to know how to get the best (God's best) out of my body-and-soul: the spirit (the wine) is willing, but the flesh (bread and water) is weak. How wonderful it will be when the spirit (I, the adopted son or daughter of God) is willing and the flesh is obedient to me! There will be my kingdom. It is mine already, but up till now I am the prince regent, not yet alone in charge. But I can tell already, I would not exchange the princedom God has given me for any other in the universe.

Prayer of a regent

Son of David, God our Father has handed over the entire kingdom, my princedom and all the others, to you as King. Train this slow, slow learner, and all of us, to cope with our own domain, but not to interfere with the domain of others, until the day when you hand the sovereignty back to our God, and he will be all in all (1 Cor 15:28). Amen.

34

The wedding banquet

Wine and weddings go together: we hardly need the story of the marriage feast at Cana to reassure us on that point, but the crisis over the running short of the wine at Cana makes a good setting for the few thoughts that follow (Jn 2).

All the New Testament, as well as the Old, in passages too many to list or quote, leads us to believe that heaven is like a wedding banquet. Who is getting married? It is the marriage between Christ, the Lamb, the bridegroom, and his bride the New Jerusalem, containing all races, all nations. At Cana, Jesus and Mary and Jesus' disciples were attending someone else's wedding. In heaven, we will in some utterly mysterious way be celebrating our own wedding.

Jesus says quite plainly (e.g., Mk 12:24) that 'when they rise from the dead, men and women do not marry'. If we think otherwise, we do not understand either the scriptures or the power of God. They do not marry one another, but in some wonderful way we shall surely not be simply celebrating someone else's marriage in heaven, but our own union with God in Christ Jesus.

Again to make a serious point in a light-hearted way, I would ask you to consider the creation myth of Aristophanes. Somewhere in the dialogues of Plato, Plato reports, maybe invents, a conversation between his master Socrates and the comic poet and playwright Aristophanes. Socrates asks the poet about the creation of the world, and Aristophanes replies with an elaborate myth of creation, which is funny enough to be a genuine fragment from the real poet. About human sexuality, he says (I quote from memory only) that God created humans first of all of a rather globular shape, and then changed his mind and split them each in two. The liberated halves ran about excitedly on their now legs, and got hopelessly mixed up before they began to yearn to get back to their other half again. Hence, says Aristophanes, human beings have to this day spent an inordinate amount of their time and energy looking for their original partners! As Christians we believe and we experience that God does not destroy his own creation; sexuality is an essential part of our human nature, and we are surely safe in believing that God will transfigure us as sexual beings, not cauterize our feelings. What this involves is another mystery, but the result will surely not leave us still searching desperately for our other half.

The wedding banquet, like all good wedding parties, must include the meeting up with all our nearest and dearest. The Song of Songs (5:6) mentions the beautiful custom of passing round the loving-cup to all the guests as well as the lovers, at a wedding feast.

But what of our enemies? Let me switch the scene to Buckingham Palace, the garden at a garden party. Suppose I have been invited. 'Very right and proper, and about time too', I say to myself smugly. But all is not well, for there are several guests there I strongly disapprove of, and I feel that Her Majesty must not know the truth, or she would never have invited them. So when she comes to shake my hand, I begin to inform her about the private life of this politican, and to bring to her notice in what bad taste that lady over there is dressed . . . and so on. What will happen? Would the Queen throw them out to oblige me, or would she not rather make a mental note never to invite me again?

Well, we *have* been invited, by the King, to his Son's wedding feast. Our fellow guests are all around us, every man, woman and child on God's earth. And the King himself is before me, listening. We must, we *must* concentrate on the astounding fact that we ourselves have been invited, and blind ourselves as earnestly as we possibly can to the sins of others. 'Father, forgive them; they do not know what they are doing.'

One last thought: women dedicated to God will not have failed to notice that there are two ways of becoming the King's daughter: one is to be adopted by the King and thus become a princess, the prince's younger sister; the other is to marry the prince.

Prayer of silence

For lovers of silence, it is good to read that there was once silence in heaven for half an hour! (Rev 8:1). Sometimes we can find no words to say to God, because he is too generous, too wonderful, we are lost for words. Thomas à Kempis in *The Imitation of Christ* says *Apud te est os meum sine voce, et silentium meum loquitur tibi*, 'Before thee my mouth is without a voice, and my silence speaks to thee'. That *can* be seen as a sad prayer, or a thoughtful prayer, but it can be a prayer of 'unutterable joy' (1 Pet 1:8), a joy so great it cannot be expressed, for it takes our breath away. Nearly thirty years ago I wrote a little poem I still love; people I have shown it to reacted by saying 'How sad!', but if you read it aright, it says rather, 'My cup is overflowing' (Ps 22[23]:5). Here is the poem:

Serenade to God

Thy balcony beckons
I sing
but my throat
has no note
my guitar has no strings.

35

A note on the Spirit

St Paul speaks of 'our whole being, spirit, soul and body' (1 Thess 5:23). Wine corresponds to spirit (Greek *pneuma*), water to soul (Greek *psyche*) and bread to body (Greek *sōma*). Body and soul together, our psycho-somatic unredeemed self, would add up only to 'flesh' (Greek *sarx*), that which is weak where the spirit is willing. God the Son in humbly mixing his wine with our bread and water himself became Spirit, soul and body, but in his case the Spirit has a capital 'S', since God the Son is a divine Person. The Holy Spirit sent by the Father and the Son is the Third Person.

We do not will ourselves into good action. Even after the resurrection the disciples did not immediately leap into action: when the Holy Spirit was sent, and not before then, those tongues of fire set their tongues on fire. By the providence of God, there is in us the capability of ignition, when that fire touches us. The Spirit breathes life into our spirit, making us children of God. We do not do it ourselves, 'it is the Spirit himself bearing witness with our spirit that we are children of God' (Rom 8:16). Our jars of stone from the earth are cup-shaped, designed originally for water, but God in Christ has changed the water into wine. Or rather, he mixes his wine with our water in such a way that the two can no longer be separated. At the breaking of bread, a fragment of bread is dropped into the chalice. There, we could say, can be seen our whole new being, body, soul and spirit, this child of God.

Prayer of one who travels in hope

Father at home, my heart is homesick for you, but I travel in hope. The weary old world through which I make my way has a saying, 'Better to travel hopefully than to arrive'. What a poisonous saying! I know quite well that things are done much better at home than they are in this place. 'One night in a bad inn', was the way St Teresa of Avila described our journey back to you.

Maybe it looked like one night for St Teresa, looking over her life. But for me I fear there are still many nights, many inns. Jesus told us, 'On the way to my Father's house there are many inns' (cf. Jn 14:2 — *pollai monai* in the Greek: many stopping-places, many stopping-off places; many *inns* is the translation of Dorothy L. Sayers). But as I go, I have my provisions for the journey, my bread, my water, my wine (cf. Judg 19:16). Not just bread and water, to keep me sternly on the path but no more than that — no, wine as well, to remind me of our city, the banquet, the home-coming. The wine gives me joy as I walk along through increasingly familiar countryside; the wine keeps me hopeful through even the darkest night.

9th of March, 1985